Modern Literature
and Christian Faith

Modern Literature
and Christian Faith

Martin Turnell

DARTON, LONGMAN & TODD

LONDON

DARTON, LONGMAN & TODD LTD.,

29A GLOUCESTER ROAD,

LONDON, S.W.7.

PN
49
.T75
1961
June 2002
ABN9348

First Published 1961

MADE AND PRINTED IN GREAT BRITAIN BY WILLIAM CLOWES AND SONS,
LIMITED, LONDON AND BECCLES. NIHIL OBSTAT: JOANNES M. T. BARTON,
S.T.D., L.S.S., CENSOR DEPUTATUS. IMPRIMATUR: E. MORROGH BERNARD,
VIC.GEN., WESTMONASTERII, DIE 27A FEBRUARII, 1961. THE NIHIL OBSTAT
AND IMPRIMATUR ARE A DECLARATION THAT A BOOK OR PAMPHLET IS
CONSIDERED TO BE FREE FROM DOCTRINAL OR MORAL ERROR. IT IS NOT
IMPLIED THAT THOSE WHO HAVE GRANTED THE NIHIL OBSTAT AND
IMPRIMATUR AGREE WITH THE CONTENTS, OPINIONS OR STATEMENTS
EXPRESSED.

NOTE

The chapters of this book originally formed the Lauriston Lectures for 1959 and the informal style of the spoken word has been retained.

CONTENTS

I THE CHANGING PATTERN

    CONTRASTS IN MODERN AND MEDIEVAL POETRY   1

II THE SHAPING OF CONTEMPORARY LITERATURE

    LAWRENCE—FORSTER—VIRGINIA WOOLF   25

III PROBLEMS OF BELIEF

    CLAUDEL—MAURIAC—GREENE   49

I

THE CHANGING PATTERN

CONTRASTS IN MODERN AND MEDIEVAL POETRY

I

On 30th October 1929 André Gide finished reading Claudel's *Satin Slipper* and recorded his opinion of it in his diary.

'I am filled with dismay,' he wrote. 'I find it difficult to believe that in any other religion Claudel's weaknesses would have flourished with the same ease as in Catholicism.'

This pungent observation focuses our attention sharply on the problem of literature and religious belief. There are two strongly conflicting views. No one supposes that belief can be a substitute for talent; but given the talent, Christians have argued that a writer's creative ability will be nourished and strengthened, his range broadened and deepened by a firmly grounded system of beliefs. Unbelievers have maintained, with equal tenacity, that any form of belief is a hindrance to the writer, that so far from nourishing his creative ability it has the reverse effect: it warps and stunts his talent, acts as blinkers which restrict or obliterate his vision. Some thirty years ago Professor I. A. Richards congratulated Mr. T. S. Eliot on effecting, in *The Waste Land*, what he described as 'a complete severance between his poetry and *all* beliefs'. Mr. Eliot replied, tartly, that he found the statement 'incomprehensible'. Whatever the opinions of the theorists, imaginative writers have seldom accepted the view that belief is inimical to creative writing. It is a matter of historical fact that in ages of settled belief men have tended to write well, and that in ages of declining belief they have gone out of their way to discover some system of belief, or some philosophy, which would provide them with a framework and give unity and shape to their artistic experience. We can add, parenthetically, that one of the difficulties about contemporary literature, one of the things that often makes it look fragmentary and confused, is precisely the fact that the writer is obliged to expend his energies in creating the conditions in which literature becomes possible instead of putting the whole of his talent into his books.

The problem of literature and belief is a complex one. The writer tries to give his reader an imaginative interpretation of the world as he sees it, or what is often called his 'vision'. The core of the problem is the relation between beliefs intellectually held and the writer's sensibility, or mode of feeling. We only get a truly Christian work of literature when the writer's whole outlook is informed by his beliefs, when we do not feel (as we do with so many contemporary Catholic writers) that intellectually held beliefs are either being imposed on experience from without, or are only very imperfectly assimilated into the experience.

While I take it as axiomatic that belief can never be a substitute for talent, I am not primarily concerned in this work to prove that one kind of literature or one writer is better than another. I simply want to describe the effect on writers of changes in belief which have taken place during the past four hundred years.

I think the period can be divided into five phases.

In the first the writer is living in a society which generally speaking is Christian. This does not mean, of course, that everyone is living an exemplary Christian life. It simply means that the writer is a member of a community which accepts the

Christian faith even if individuals do not always practise it, that his work is a reflection of the communal outlook even if he is not dealing with a specifically Christian subject, that his conception of the nature of man is basically Christian.

In the second phase there is a break in the pattern. The community is divided into a large number of warring factions and conflicting outlooks. The Church is replaced by the churches; Theology by the theologies; Philosophy by the philosophies; Science by the sciences. The literature of this phase is dominated by a feeling of unrest, by the writer's sense of living in an age of crisis.

A third phase might be called the Age of Compromise. It is, as we shall see, the period of the Counter-Reformation and Baroque art. The Christian artist tries to come to terms with the new experience and new insights released by the up-heavals of the previous century.

In the fourth phase literature divides into two main classes: religious and secular. The Christian writer, so far from feeling himself a member of a homogeneous society, is very clearly a member of a minority, and his work is coloured by his isolation.

In the final phase, the sense of belonging to a minority is transformed into the sense of belonging to the opposition. It is in this phase, as I shall try to show, that an internal conflict seems to arise between the writer's artistic experience and a religion which is held intellectually.

I have never cared for abstractions. I have never been able to feel much enthusiasm for the sort of abstract debate which raged with such fury in France a quarter of a century ago about 'the purity of the source' and 'the sanctity of truth'. It seems to me that the discussion of the problem of literature and belief can only serve any useful purpose if it is firmly based on concrete examples. In this first chapter, I give a broad and necessarily simplified picture of some of the main changes that have taken place between the sixteenth and the twentieth centuries illustrated by quotations from six poets. In chapter two I examine the effect of the absence of belief on the work of three twentieth-century novelists. In the final chapter I look at the work of three contemporary Catholic writers. I shall then try to draw some general conclusions.

I shall begin by comparing passages from representative medieval and modern poems. The first passage comes from Chaucer's *Prologue*, the second from Eliot's *Waste Land*. This is Chaucer:

> Whan that Aprillë with his shourës sote
> The droghte of Marche hath percèd to the rote,
> And bathèd every veyne in swich licour,
> Of which vertu engendrèd is the flour;
> Whan Zephirus eek with his swetë breeth
> Inspirèd hath in every holt and heeth
> The tendre croppès and the yongë sonne
> Hath in the Ram his halfë cours y-ronne,
> And smalë fowlës maken melodye,
> That slepen al the night with open yë,
> (So priketh hem nature in hir corages):
> Than longen folk to goon on pilgrimages
> (And palmers for to seken straungë strondes)
> To fernë halwës, couthe in sondry londes;
> And specially, from every shirës end
> Of Engelond, to Caunterbury they wende,
> The holy blisful martir for to seke,
> That hem hath holpen, whan that they were seke.

This is Eliot:

> April is the cruellest month, breeding
> Lilacs out of the dead land, mixing
> Memory and desire, stirring
> Dull roots with spring rain.
> Winter kept us warm, covering
> Earth in a forgetful snow, feeding
> A little life with dried tubers.

The first difference is the contrast between Chaucer's spontaneous joy in the created world—we remember the gorgeous Wife of Bath's enthusiastic plea for 'octogamye'—and the mixture of horror and disgust with which Eliot regards it. In one, harmony and stability: in the other immense uncertainty and unrest; Chaucer rejoicing in something possessed, Eliot overwhelmed by a sense of something irrevocably lost. This is apparent in the details of the passages. Both writers are describing changes that occur in nature with the coming of spring. It is a time of awakening, and for the medieval poet awakening means an increase of life, a joyful release from the bondage of winter. April showers are 'sweet', and their virtue is to break up the winter-bound earth; they bring flowers and the fruits of the earth; the crops are 'tender', the sun 'young'. For Eliot, on the contrary, April is 'the cruellest month' precisely because it is the end of winter and the beginning of change from insensibility to awakening. Winter is not, as it was for Chaucer, a time of death but of pleasant numbness and insensibility. It is an awakening from which the poet would gladly escape. All that the earth produces is a few lilacs whose pale fragility is thrown into relief by the neutral background of the wilderness. The roots are 'dull', unwilling to grow. Chaucer is sensitive enough to the effects of the spring. Birds sing and cannot sleep. Men are revived by the stimulus of the season, are restless and feel the need to travel after being shut up all winter. In Eliot the effects of spring are narrowly sexual. It brings memories which stir sluggish desires, but there is none of the gaiety suggested by Chaucer's singing birds: it is an unhappy, morbid state. While Chaucer's is a poetry of acceptance, Eliot's by comparison is a poetry of refusal and as such represents the modern outlook as Chaucer's represents the medieval.

Perhaps the most striking thing about the two passages is the difference of focus. The medieval poet is interested primarily in *things*, and his poem is a record of his reactions to them. The balance of the poem comes from the close correspondence between emotion and the object which evokes it. In the modern poet the process is reversed. The poem is an analysis of a state of mind and the connection with spring, and the use of a vocabulary drawn from spring, in a way fortuitous and subjective. In other words, the poet is not describing spring or even his sensations in spring: he is equating spring awakening with a particular mood, and simply uses images drawn from spring to exteriorise certain very personal feelings.

I must emphasise again that I am not concerned with the relative merits of the two passages. I am not saying that Chaucer is better than Eliot, or Eliot better than Chaucer. I am not saying that Eliot is not a great poet, or is an 'escapist'. I think he is a great poet, and that his greatness is apparent in the unflinching honesty with which he faces a tragic situation. It is this honesty, or so it seems to me, that gives his finest

verse its peculiar toughness and resilence. All that I am concerned with is the contrasting attitudes of the two poets
towards their world. It is evident that Chaucer's work is the
product of a young civilisation. This explains the simplicity
and directness of his reactions. The simplicity and uncom-
plicated reactions are reflected in the straightforward syntax
and the number of active verbs: 'percèd', 'bathèd', 'in-
spirèd', 'wende'. They are also reflected in the difference
between Chaucer's 'longen' and Eliot's 'memory'. The
pilgrims' 'longing' to take to the road is prompted by
memories, but they are pleasant memories which lead to
action, lead them to plunge lightheartedly once again into the
active, open-air life: there is none of the *passive* nostalgia that
is evident in Eliot's 'memory'. There is a marked difference,
too, between Chaucer's fondness for the active verb and
Eliot's reliance on present participles—there are five of them
in seven lines—on those dragging, wistful present participles
which paradoxically have the effect of binding the passage together, giving it its personal tautness and strength, while at
the same time conveying an almost suffocating sense of
resignation.

This brings me to a final point. For Chaucer's bawdy pilgrims the expedition to Canterbury was no doubt an excuse
for a 'jaunt', and certainly piety plays little part in the tales
that they exchange. Nevertheless, they are on a pilgrimage.
In this sense, the poem can be regarded as an allegory of the
Christian life. For the Christian life is essentially a pilgrimage;
all Chaucer's characters are moving towards a known goal.
It is this which distinguishes them from the characters in
modern poems. Travel bulks large in the literature written
during the past century, but the pilgrim of Chaucer or

Bunyan has been replaced by the tourist who has no fixed goal and travels for the fun of the journey, in the hope of running into adventures or simply because he cannot sit still. In nineteenth-century France the traveller is always looking wistfully backwards over his shoulder towards the 'lost paradise' of childhood which had become the symbol of unity and security: a vanished unity and a security that had gone. The travellers in Baudelaire's poem *Le Voyage* find themselves pursuing a moving goal, a mirage which leads them on and gets them nowhere, while in Eliot's poem the journey is a circular tour of the Waste Land, a spiritual stocktaking which ends with a depressing balance sheet where everything is in the red, and there is only a mark of interrogation beyond.

I think that we can say that the value of medieval poetry, the value of Dante or Chaucer or Langland, different as they are in outlook and stature, lies to a very considerable degree in the feeling of stability and confidence, in the belief in a fixed unchanging order, a world with a heaven above and a hell beneath, which they succeed in communicating to the reader. I am going to suggest that the appeal of later poets lies in something which is the opposite of this, that it lies in a sense of the dissolution of the old world, in the loss of unity.

For at the Renaissance the stability which pervades almost every line written by Dante or Chaucer was destroyed for a large section of European society. The old world had come to an end: a new world was beginning. It is true that the Renaissance made discoveries about man, about the external world, but its enormous delight in nature and in man involved a sundering of God and man who had been joined in the Incarnation, of nature and the supernatural. There is a feeling that nature and man are both independent of anything outside them, and in consequence a failure to relate experience to unchanging principles which had been natural to the medieval mind.

This view has been stated in a striking article by George Santayana called 'The Absence of Religion in Shakespeare'. He finds that Shakespeare is 'remarkable among the greater poets for being without a philosophy and without a religion'. 'In his drama', he goes on, 'there is no fixed conception of any forces, natural or moral, dominating our mortal energies.' He concludes from this that 'we can hardly find in Shakespeare all that the highest poet could give'.

I doubt whether contemporary Shakespearean critics would accept this view without considerable qualifications, but as a general account of what occurred after the break-up of the medieval synthesis it seems to me to be valid. I do not propose to discuss Shakespeare: he is too big to serve as an example. I propose instead to look at another poet. A great poet certainly, but not a poet of the calibre of Shakespeare. I mean John Donne.

If Donne was one of the most important poets of his century, it was because he was at once the last scholastic and the first of the moderns. In his work two worlds meet with a difference. For Donne lived in an age of transition from the medieval to the modern worlds. It is a change from a state of spiritual unity to the dualism of the contemporary world. One critic has spoken of his poetry as 'the battle-ground of the difficulty of belief and the reluctance to doubt'.

This puts the matter extremely well. Donne was one of the first poets to find himself obliged to choose between conflicting outlooks, for whom a choice of outlook was a major issue. There had been differences of opinion in the Middle

Ages, but differences within a single philosophy. From Donne onwards a difference of opinion means a complete difference of outlook. He was born a Catholic and became an Anglican. He had Catholicism in his blood and did not find it easy to throw over the inherited habits of mind and ways of feeling of innumerable generations. He himself was very conscious of the difficulty. In 1615, only a few months after his ordination, he said in a remarkable letter to Sir Henry Godere:

'You shall seldom see a coyne, upon which the stamp were removed, though to imprint a better, but it looks awry and squint. And so, for the most part, do minds which have received divers impressions. I will not, nor need to you, compare the Religions. The channels of Gods mercies run through both fields; and they are sister teats of his graces, yet both diseased and infected, but not both alike.'

From this we can turn to the famous sonnet written three years later:

Show me deare Christ, thy Spouse, so bright and clear,
What! is it She, which on the other shore
Goes richly painted? or which rob'd and tore
Laments and mournes in Germany and here?
Sleepes she a thousand, then peepes up one year?
Is she selfe truth and errs? now new, now outwore?
Doth she, and did she, and shall she evermore
On one, on seaven, or on no hill appeare?
Dwells she with us, or like adventuring knights
First travaile we to seeke and then make Love?
Betray kind husband thy spouse to our sights,
And let myne amorous soule court thy mild Dove,
Who is most trew, and most pleasing to thee, then
When she'is embrac'd and open to most men.

This is not by any means among the best of Donne's religious poems. There is an element of frivolity in the comparison between the believer and 'adventuring knights' pursuing a reluctant mistress, which recalls some of the more cynical of the *Songs and Sonets*. But it does reflect, as surely as the letter to Sir Henry Godere, the perplexity of the man of goodwill in the seventeenth century who is trying to discover the source of truth. What is notable about both letter and sonnet is not so much the attitude of moderation and toleration, as the implication that there is no one church which is the repository of truth, that each of them has its points, but that each is in some degree 'diseased and infected'.

It should now be possible to draw some tentative conclusions. When I said that the value of medieval literature lies in its power of communicating a feeling of stability and confidence, I was not forgetting that Dante lived in a politically divided world, or that Langland was Chaucer's contemporary. There was tension enough in the Middle Ages and an instance nearer home—Gerard Manley Hopkins—shows that Catholicism does not exclude tension. We have to distinguish between writers who are outside the tension and those who are inside it. Beneath the clash recorded by Dante, beneath Villon's lament for lost beauty, beneath the apparent disunity of Hopkins, there is an underlying unity. Their unrest is related to a background of harmony as Donne's is not. With Donne we meet, perhaps for the first time, that divided self which is characteristic of modern poetry. He expresses for the first time the writer's awareness of living in an age of spiritual crisis, and it is this awareness which dominates a great deal of the most significant poetry written since his day. The scene shifts, there are variations, apparent changes of emphasis, but at bottom the crisis is the same. Donne's work is the more intense because he was at the point at which the break took place. The unity which was destroyed was real for him, not simply an inherited memory, a lost paradise as it is for the contemporary poet.

The change from a theocentric to an anthropocentric world, the tendency of man to regard himself and his world as self-subsistent and self-sufficient, the wholesale glorification of the visible world, which were among the results of the Renaissance, clearly presented religious people with a problem. What in fact was the attitude of the Christian to be towards the new humanism? He naturally disapproved of it in so far as it was pagan, but he could not be blind to its positive virtues. The Church has always claimed that she can assimilate anything that is good or true in other systems. That is what the artists of the Age of Baroque attempted to do. They tried to harness the vitality released by the Renaissance, and it does indeed become almost tangible in the immense angels of Baroque sculpture and the flying draperies which envelop its saints.

The readiness to accept, to assimilate, to transform is reflected in the differences between medieval and Baroque art. In a medieval work like the carvings at Chartres the emphasis falls on two themes: Creation and Incarnation. The men who made them could not of course omit all reference to the 'sorrowful mysteries', but it is confined to a glimpse of the foot of the Cross and a couple of Nails on one of the porticoes. It is not until the seventeenth century that the Crucifixion becomes the centre of religious art, that poetry and painting drip with the Blood of Christ and the martyrs. Now the

Counter-Reformation made one distinctive contribution to religious art. The brilliant ornate churches, the statues of saints swooning in ecstasy with distorted features and writhing limbs, the poetry where an immense exuberance threatens to burst through language, was the last conscious attempt to hold the balance between spirit and flesh. It was intended not merely to startle and impress, not merely as a protest against the gloomy iconoclasm of the Protestant north; it was intended to attract the unbeliever into the gay fantastic churches to marvel in the hope that he would remain to pray. It was an extraordinary performance certainly, but it was the product of a divided Europe. We feel already that the artist had an axe to grind, that he was trying to prove something.

He was trying to prove something, but not by argument or the methods of the schoolmen. He was trying to put across an experience which would *compete* with the humanists on their own ground. He was also using them as allies in the struggle against Protestantism and the Lutheran view of the consequences of the Fall of Man. In its discovery of the Natural Man, the Renaissance had insisted on the pleasures of the eye and ear, the senses of touch, taste and smell. It wanted to satisfy the senses which seemed to have been starved by medieval asceticism. The Baroque artist tried to do the same thing through religion, tried to create a Religious Man who was far nearer to the Natural Man of the Renaissance than to the medieval ascetic.

It is not surprising that men living in a period of religious upheaval should have been preoccupied with sin and suffering, that their minds should have been dominated by the figure of the suffering Christ rather than by that of the glorious or the triumphant Christ. Yet it would clearly be untrue to say that the seventeenth century was exclusively preoccupied with suffering, and the paintings and statues of saints in ecstasy are there to prove the contrary. The answer lies deeper than that. The artists discovered that representations of suffering, ecstasy, and death were much better calculated to serve their purpose. They could be made to appeal to the senses. They could be represented not merely in words, but in paint and stone. The first result was the tendency of the different arts to merge into one another, to approximate to the visual arts. In the Middle Ages sculpture had been formal: it had shown the Christian Saint rather than a particular saint. In the seventeenth century it became highly realistic. The sculptor tried to represent movement, to probe into man's deepest and most intimate experiences, to catch and hold the actual instant of ecstasy or death, as Bernini did in his St. Teresa or his Blessed Ludovica Albertoni, as El Greco did in his painting of Pentecost.

All this is true of the poetry of the period, particularly of Crashaw's. It is extremely rich in visual, concrete, physical images. Not merely one, but all five senses are solicited on every page, almost in every line. In his rendering of Aquinas's *Adoro te devote*, for example, we read:

> O soft self-wounding Pelican!
> Whose breast weepes Balm for wounded man.
> Ah this way bend thy benign floud
> To'a bleeding Heart that gaspes for blood:
> That blood, whose least drops soveraign be
> To wash my worlds of sins from me.

Aquinas's *Pie pellicane* is transformed into a 'soft self-wounding Pelican' which does not merely bleed, but 'weepes'

blood for another wounded, bleeding heart which 'gaspes'
for still more blood.

The Divine Epigram on the text 'Blessed be the paps which
Thou hast sucked' is much more startling:

> Suppose He had been tabled at thy teats,
> Thy hunger feels not what He eats;
> He'll have His teat ere long, a bloody one,
> The mother then must suck the son.

Small wonder that Mr. Aldous Huxley once remarked that
some Baroque art makes us feel that we have walked into a
room at the wrong moment.

I think that the Baroque artists must have known that they
could not communicate the actual vision of the saint in
ecstasy, or describe what happens at the moment of death.
They also knew that ecstasy and death had marked physiological repercussions. They tried by a realistic representation
of the physiological aspects to get as close as possible to the
content of experience. In the end this involved a more and
more determined appeal to the senses in the attempt—the
impossible attempt—to reach through the senses something
which lay outside the field of sense-perception.

I want to make a jump now of two hundred years and glance
briefly at a much more extreme example of compromise. I
want to describe what happens when the attempt to assimilate
is pushed to the point at which the thing assimilated becomes
the true substance of the poem, and is simply covered with a
veneer of religion.

Coventry Patmore is one of the more curious figures among
English nineteenth-century poets. He married three times.

He is said by his grandson to have fallen physically in love with Alice Meynell when he was over seventy. In addition to a handsomely bound edition of the works of Aquinas, a complete set of a work called the *Eroticon Biblion* was among the treasures of his library. He tried, in a sequence of poems called *To the Unknown Eros*, to work out a sort of parallel between the union of God and His Church and the union of two people in marriage. This has won for him considerable favour among Catholic writers as a mystical poet.

His pre-conversion poem on married love, *The Angel in the House*, is of small literary value, but it provides one or two good laughs. Opening the poem at random, we come across this gem of Victorian complacency which occurs in a conversation between the hero of the piece and his future father-in-law who is an Anglican dean. The young man has just asked the dean for his daughter's hand:

> He gave
> His glad consent, if I could get
> Her love. A dear, good Girl! she'd have
> Only three thousand pounds as yet;
> More bye and bye.

'His writings are never dull', remarks the editor of the Oxford edition in an introduction which must rank as one of the curiosities of modern criticism. Superficially, the versification of *To the Unknown Eros* may appear more virile. Yet if we compare it with the genuine vitality of the mature Hopkins we see at once that the appearance of tautness, which is seldom maintained, depends not on rhythm, but on a harsh, awkward syntax, and on irritating habits of inversion and elision. It reveals the same prolixity that we find in

nearly all Victorian verse, and the same poetic clichés. Nor
can we be impressed by the alleged profundity of the psychology of love. When we come to the end of an ode, we cannot
help remarking how very little has in fact been said. And
nothing can compensate us for the ugly, gritty syntax.

In *Eros and Psyche* we read:

> O, heavenly Lover true,
> Is this thy mouth upon my forehead press'd?
> Are these thine arms about my bosom link'd?
> Are these thy hands that tremble near my heart?
> Where join two hearts, for juncture more distinct?
> By thee and by my maiden zone caress'd,
> What dim, waste tracts of life shine sudden, like moonbeams
> On windless ocean shaken by sweet dreams!

The construction of the last three lines defeats me, but I
am in no doubt about the significance of 'my maiden zone
caress'd', or of the 'juncture more distinct'. What is curious
is the mixture of these crudely sexual images and the tiresome poetic jargon of the time: the 'bosom', 'moonbeams',
'sweet dreams', and the rest. The poem goes on:

> Ah, stir not to depart!
> Kiss me again, thy Wife and Virgin too!
> O love, that, like a rose,
> Deckest my breast with beautiful repose,
> Kiss me again, and clasp me round the heart,
> Till filled with thee am I
> As the cocoon is with the butterfly!

We know that Patmore purported to establish some sort of
relation or parallel between the union of God with the soul
and the union of man and woman in marriage. His theory is

proudly produced by his apologists with suitably fulsome commendation. Clearly the odes can be read in this way, but the crucial point is where the emphasis lies. For myself, I can only say that Patmore's religious allegory has a very sexual underneath. His 'Virgin' is singularly out of place with that very phallic rose, and the still more phallic butterfly.

In *Aureas of Delight* he wrote:

> I, with heart-quake
> Dreaming or thinking of that realm of Love
> See, oft, a dove
> Tangled in frightful nuptials with a snake . . .

This throws an essential light on his failure and on the failure of his age. Underneath the tiresome clichés and the conventional sentiments there was both ability and vision. But there was something badly wrong with their minds, and the result was not poetry but a mess. For the 'frightful nuptials with a snake' and 'the tortur'd knot' of the next line belong to the Victorian nightmare. It was a very Freudian nightmare, but it seems best to recognise it for what it was instead of trying to hide poetic failure by fanciful theories of divine and human love. It is at least a possible view that rather than being 'a great Catholic poet' his principal characteristic was obsession with sexuality.

It is commonly but mistakenly assumed that the primary function of religious poetry is to provide the reader with some form of transcendental experience, and literary critics have contracted the bad habit of describing almost any poetry with a religious theme as 'mystical'. Poetry is a human activity. We expect religious poetry to interpret life in terms of religion certainly, but we also expect religion to *conserve* the natural human instincts. Now one of the most disquieting things about modern religious poetry is the failure of the poet's religion to do precisely that. Patmore is one example. Francis Thompson is another. Thompson, one feels, was a man whose best instincts had collapsed. His religion was a temptation instead of a discipline. It encouraged him to import into his verse the worst and shoddiest emotional clichés of the day, and was in the last analysis indistinguishable from a decadent religiosity which was fashionable in the eighties and nineties.

Hopkins was a great poet because his religion did enable him to resist the disintegrating forces of his time. It was responsible for the freshness and vitality of his language which relate him to Shakespeare and distinguish him from his Victorian contemporaries. Nearly all his critics have commented on the sensuous element in his work, but there is something essentially vital and alive about his descriptions of nature: a sense of things living and growing which is the opposite of the hot-house blooms of Thompson or Patmore's queer, drooping, sexy azaleas. I have quoted some examples of Patmore's contorted syntax. When we turn to Hopkins's we find by contrast that it possesses a genuine, sinewy tautness:

> No worst, there is none. Pitched past pitch of grief,
> More pangs will, schooled at forepangs, wilder wring . . .

In these lines the words are literally wrung out of the poet by the intensity of his agony. The alliteration in the first line is immensely effective in giving the language its extraordinary density: 'Pitched past pitch of grief . . .', while the inserted clause in the second line, separating the auxiliary from its infinitive, produces the sense of flexibility and vigour.

Consider again this description of the nun on board the sinking *Deutschland*:

> The ra*s*h *s*mart *s*loggering *b*rine
> *B*linds her . . .

There is nothing 'poetic' in the derogatory sense about the unexpected adjectives 'rash' and 'smart', or the immensely effective 'sloggering' with its obvious Anglo-Saxon antecedents. We have an acute physical sensation of the cold, biting water violently hurled against the solitary figure, which is heightened by the alliteration—another ancient device—and the enjambment.

Hopkins was a great poet who made no concessions to the age, but his work nevertheless does not entirely escape the general limitation that we find in nearly all post-Reformation religious poetry. We can say, with Dante and Chaucer and Villon in mind, that in the Middle Ages religious poetry was not a special department of poetry: religion extended instead of limiting the poet's range. In the modern world religious poetry tends more and more to become a special branch of poetry, and the poet thinks of himself as an isolated figure. He thinks of himself as the spokesman either of a particular religious body as Crashaw and Herbert—the Catholic and the Anglican did—, or as the champion of Christianity waging a lonely war against the forces of secularism. *Paradise Regained* is not a Christian epic: it is the epic of Protestant modernism and the voice is the strident voice of a president of the Modern Churchman's Union. Racine's *Athalie* is the drama of the Jansenist fighting a losing battle on two fronts against political despotism and the machinations of the Society of Jesus. There is a third group—the group which includes Donne's *Holy Sonnets*, the best of Hopkins and a poem like Eliot's *Little Gidding*—in which the poet is concerned less with the interpretation of life in terms of a universal religion than with the expression of a personal religious drama.

II

THE SHAPING OF CONTEMPORARY
LITERATURE

LAWRENCE—FORSTER—VIRGINIA WOOLF

II

'NI ange ni bête', said Pascal. This was the Christian conception of the nature of man. He belonged partly to the spiritual, and partly to the animal worlds. He was imperfect, but was endowed with reason. He was engaged in a constant struggle to control his animal instincts and to preserve a state of equilibrium, or to transcend his animal instincts and advance in the way of perfection. Since the Renaissance, writers have tended to concentrate on conflict or tension. In his own century Pascal's formula was re-stated in different terms. There was a conflict between 'love and honour', between 'duty and inclination', or simply between reason and impulse. We are inclined to think of the eighteenth century as the Age of Reason, but this is a simplification. What really happened in the eighteenth century was that the conflict was largely eliminated by dividing man into two or, to put it in another way, by exteriorising the conflict. The century was dominated not by the divided modern man, but by the twin figures of the Man of Feeling and the Rational Man. The Man of Feeling believed that emotion was good and should be given free rein: the Rational Man shared the belief of the age in the perfectibility of human nature, but thought that the good life was to be achieved by the exercise of reason untrammelled by emotion.

Although the Man of Feeling and the Rational Man appear to be antithetical types, it was their joint operations which sapped the foundations of civilisation and prepared the way for the French Revolution. The immediate effect of the Revolution was to sweep away rational controls and release the violent impulses which until the end of the eighteenth century had been held in check. In Balzac man is reduced to a 'temperament', in Zola to what he called an 'appetite'. Zola's contribution to the debate on the nature of man was not a very original one, but it was a very important factor in determining the shape of contemporary literature. What he did was to simplify Balzac's already simplified psychology, give his 'monomaniacs' a pseudo-scientific basis, and launch the result as 'the Physiological Man'. The short answer to Pascal was contained in the three words of the title of one of his novels: 'la bête humaine'.

The nineteenth century was essentially an Age of Revolution. The French Revolution which inaugurated it was followed by a series of revolutions which affected every sphere of life: they were religious, political, industrial and scientific. Yet the nineteenth century in its own way reproduced the conflicts which are apparent in the seventeenth and eighteenth centuries. The French Revolution was the immediate cause of the flowering of Romanticism not merely in France, but in England and Germany. Romanticism has been out of favour for a number of years. There are certainly grounds on which it can be criticised. Baudelaire touched on one of its fundamental weaknesses when he spoke of it as the Romantic 'insurrection', and Professor Weidlé when he described it as 'the death of a style'. The nineteenth century was undoubtedly one of the greatest ages of European literature, but there is nothing that can be described accurately as 'the nineteenth-century style', as we can justifiably speak of 'the seventeenth-century style', or 'the eighteenth-century style'. This is perhaps more evident in France than in England. The English are allergic to abstract thought and to theorising about the arts: the French adore it. What we find in France is a large number of movements, but more obviously a very large number of conflicting aesthetic theories. Not merely Romanticism, but Realism, Naturalism, Impressionism, Symbolism, even something hideously known as 'Decadentism'.

If the French Revolution was a rebellion against a social order which had become effete, the Romantic Movement in all three countries was a rebellion against a classicism which had lost its driving power and hardened into dogmatism, had become a matter of rules and little else. It is of the essence of revolutions that they are destructive, that they do not normally lead to a fresh order, but to chaos and despotism. This is true of Romanticism in so far as it did not help to produce a ninteenth-century style, but it did have a positive contribution to make to literature. What it chiefly did in literature was to release many new insights: those insights which had been suppressed beneath eighteenth-century decorum and which had caused outbreaks of madness in poets like Cowper and Smart, and something akin to madness in Dr. Johnson's famous melancholy.

The release of the new insights coupled with the failure of the revolutionary movements to create a new order gives the literature of the century one of its distinguishing characteristics. We find these new insights developing outside the Christian tradition; we find a hunger for some form of transcendental experience completely divorced from institutional religion or, indeed, combined with hostility to institutional religion as such. This produced a form of experience which

Professor Zaehner describes as 'praeternatural' to distinguish it from religious mysticism. The examples are many: the 'nature mysticism' of Wordsworth, Blake's prophetic books, the experience of Gérard de Nerval, Rimbaud and Proust in France or, in our own century, the very profound insights of D. H. Lawrence. There is clearly a good deal of truth in T. E. Hulme's definition of Romanticism as 'spilt religion'. For there is not the slightest doubt that experience which once found an outlet within the framework of revealed religion emerged instead in a form of literature which was a substitute for religion. In the words of Jacques Rivière: 'Literature came to be regarded as a raid on the absolute and its results as a revelation.'

This brings me back to the conflict which runs through the nineteenth century and to the nature of man. It is a fair inference that you cannot have a literature without some philosophical assumptions even though the writer is unconscious of them. The nineteenth century was divided between two philosophical systems which both stemmed from the eighteenth century. One was the scientific determinism which came from the thinkers of the Enlightenment: the other was the philosophical idealism which derives from Kant. Until the latter part of the eighteenth century man had believed very firmly in the reality of the external world. Then he began to doubt. His doubts increased as the century wore on, and they led him to doubt his own existence. At the root of all modern philosophies there is a pronounced subjective element. We cannot say with certainty whether idealism was prompted by the desire to escape from a purely mechanical universe, or whether determinism asserted the existence of material reality so vehemently in order to allay the doubts created by

28

idealism, but there was clearly an interplay between them. The antithesis idealism-determinism corresponds in the literary order to the antithesis Romanticism-Classicism and their derivatives. These derivatives were Impressionism, Symbolism and *Surréalisme* on the one hand: Realism, Naturalism and the various forms of political art such as Socialist Realism, on the other. Idealism leads to an exclusive concentration on inner experience, to the hunt for what one of Proust's critics has called the *état privilégié*: the supreme moment of the Romantics, 'the moment that never returns' of the Impressionists, or what both Rimbaud and Proust described as *la vraie vie*—the reality hidden behind the deceptive appearance of things. Determinism produces the minute inventory of material reality that we find in the Realists and Naturalists, an endless preoccupation with the physical appearances of men and buildings as the sole reality in a world of dissolving values. Both lead to an impoverishment of the nature of man. In the novels of personal relationships characters are reduced to phantoms, in Impressionist paintings to featureless blobs of colour on the landscape: in the work of the Naturalists man becomes a robot, in the political novel one of the herd, a cog in the party machine. One produces an art which is a substitute for religion; the other a completely secularised art.

I have spoken at some length about what happened in France at the beginning of the nineteenth century. I have done so because the tendencies I have described were to shape the literature of our own century not only in France but in this country. What one may call the shaping power simply happened to be more clearly discernible in France than in any other country.

I am now going to re-cross the Channel and look at three twentieth-century English writers: D. H. Lawrence, E. M. Forster, and Virginia Woolf.

There has been considerable argument both about Lawrence's status and about the kind of writer he was. It has been suggested, for example, that though he possessed genius and excelled in descriptions of the English landscape, he was not really a novelist at all. I do not share this view. Although he was a magnificent literary critic, a poet of distinction, and the author of some important works like *Fantasia of the Unconscious* which are admittedly somewhat difficult to classify, I propose to treat him primarily as a novelist. Although the novels are already beginning to wear a period air and though there is an unmistakable flavour of the 'twenties about them, Lawrence seems to me to be one of the greatest masters of prose fiction who have written in English in the present century. If he was a great artist, he was also, as great artists usually are, a moralist. Dr. Leavis has put it very well. Lawrence's fiction, he said, is both an *experience* and an *experiment*. He was immensely preoccupied with the effect on man of what he called the disintegrating forces of modern life. The aim of his novels was to discover a new mode of consciousness. But the novels are in no sense *romans à thèse*. He tried to discover the new mode of consciousness by methods which are proper to the artist: they are not moral treatises cast in the form of fiction. That is what Dr. Leavis meant when he said that they were both an 'experience' and and an 'experiment'.

Lawrence's own view of the function of the novel is stated most succinctly in *Lady Chatterley's Lover*:

'It is the way our sympathy flows and recoils [he said] that really determines our lives. And here lies the vast importance of the novel, properly handled. It can inform and lead into new places the flow of our sympathetic consciousness, and it can lead our sympathy away in recoil from things gone dead. Therefore, the novel, properly handled, can reveal the most secret places of life; for it is in the *passional* secret places of life, above all, that the tide of sensitive awareness needs to ebb and flow, cleansing and freshening.'

In an essay on Edgar Allan Poe in *Studies in Classic American Literature*, he described the rhythm of American art-activity as dual. There is, he said, 'a disintegrating and sloughing off of the old consciousness' and 'the forming of a new consciousness underneath'. I can imagine no better description of his own work. For the rhythm of his greatest novels—I am thinking of *The Rainbow* and *Women in Love*—is essentially dual. Man struggles against the disintegrating forces of contemporary life, but he tries all the time to forge a fresh mode of consciousness. In *The Rainbow* we are told of one of the central characters:

'He too was at the end of his desires. He had done the things he wanted to. They had all ended in a disintegrated lifelessness of soul, which he hid under a tolerant good humour. He no longer cared about anything on earth, neither man nor woman, nor God nor humanity. He had come to a stability of nullification. He did not care any more, neither about his own body nor his soul. Only he would preserve intact his own life. Only the simple, superficial fact of living persisted.'

From this we can turn to a more general picture of modern life in the same novel:

'The place had the strange desolation of a ruin. Colliers

hanging about in gangs and groups, or passing along asphalt pavements heavily to work, seemed not like living people, but like spectres. The rigidity of the blank streets, the homogeneous amorphous sterility of the whole place suggested death rather than life. There was no meeting place, no centre, no artery, no organic function. There it lay, like the new foundations of a red-brick confusion rapidly spreading, like a skin-disease . . . the place was a moment of chaos perpetuated . . . The terrible gaunt repose of the miners' bearing fascinated her. Like creatures with no more hope, within some utterly un-living shell they passed meaninglessly along, with strange isolated dignity.'

The symbols of death and meaninglessness stand out: 'disintegrated lifelessness of soul'; 'stability of nullification'; 'spectres'; 'rigidity of the blank streets'; 'homogeneous amorphous sterility'; 'moment of chaos perpetuated'. No other modern writer has stated the predicament of man cut off from his roots—his spiritual roots—with such power.

Although Lawrence's genius is very evident in his descriptions of strange states of consciousness, he is like most modern writers less impressive when he attempts a statement of his positives. This passage comes from *The Woman Who Rode Away*:

'But at this time her commonplace consciousness was numb, she was aware of her immediate surroundings as shadows, almost immaterial. With refined and heightened senses she could hear the sound of the earth winging on its journey, like a shot arrow, the rippling of the air, and the boom of the great arrowstring'.

In a passage in *Women in Love* describing the relations of Birkin, who is Lawrence's spokesman, and Ursula, we read:

'It was a perfect passing away for both of them, and at the same time the most intolerable accession into being, the marvellous fulness of immediate gratification, overwhelming, outflooding from the source of the deepest life-force, the darkest, deepest, strangest life-source of the human body, at the back and base of the loins.'

It is of the essence of such passages that the writer seems to be straining—the strain is apparent in the vocabulary and repetitions of the second passage—to reach states which lie not simply beyond the range of words, but beyond the natural range of human experience. It is also of the essence of these states that they are transient as well as elusive.

The commonest criticism of Lawrence is that he was obsessed with the idea of sexual union, that he indulged in a sort of *mystique* of the blood and of sexuality. I think that there is at least some justice in these criticisms, that they explain both the dramatic nature of his work and the fundamental contradiction which lies at the heart of it. The trouble with most of his characters is that they cannot love. What he describes in *The Rainbow* and still more in *Women in Love* is a dreadful, destructive love–hate relationship. This is what happens to the wonderful love of Will Brangwen and Anna in *The Rainbow*:

'This is what their love had become, a sensuality violent as death. They had no conscious intimacy, no tenderness of love. It was all the lust and the infinite maddening intoxication of the senses, a passion of death.'

In *Women in Love* he is equally downright:

'The hot, narrow intimacy between man and wife was abhorrent.'

'On the whole he hated sex, it was such a limitation. It was sex that turned man into a broken half of a couple . . .'

In *Fantasia of the Unconscious* the contradiction is admitted:

'Sex holds *two* people together: but it tends to disintegrate society unless it is subordinated to the great male passion of collective purpose.'

'Assert sex as the predominant fulfilment, and you get the collapse of living purpose in man.'

The admission is plain enough. He sought some kind of transcendental experience—it is the supreme moment of the Romantics again—through human relations, but the experiment always ended in failure. We are fobbed off with abstractions: 'great male passion of collective purpose', 'collapse of living purpose'. For Lawrence looked for something absolute in a realm where, in the nature of things, it could not exist. When sex failed he tried to cut himself off from humanity, tried to found a new race in Mexico. And that was a failure too. His career recalls in a curious way Rimbaud's. In the *Illuminations* Rimbaud, too, tried to discover a 'new mode of consciousness', but there was no framework to give shape and pattern to his experience. He realised that he was heading for madness. He was obliged, as he himself put it in *Une Saison en enfer*, to return to 'rugged reality'. Yet instead of pursuing his experiments as Lawrence did, he abandoned poetry and went to Abyssinia, not to found a new race but to do some gun-running.

E. M. Forster is a very distinguished novelist, but he is not a writer of the same calibre as Lawrence. He has written five novels and one volume of short stories. Four of the novels and the collection of short stories were published between 1905 and 1914: *A Passage to India* appeared in 1924. I am mainly concerned here with *Howards End*, which was published in 1910, and *A Passage to India*. Both these books deal with the end of a world: *Howards End* with the world that disappeared after the First World War; *A Passage to India* with the end of British imperialism. Mr. Forster's distinction as a novelist lies very largely in his sensitive appreciation of what was gracious and valuable in the old world, and in the honesty with which he recognises that its values were insufficient to hold it together.

'We are not concerned with the very poor [he remarks ironically in *Howards End*]. They are unthinkable, and only to be approached by the statistician or the poet. This story deals with gentle folk, or with those who are obliged to pretend that they are gentle folk.'

The characters are divided into two contrasted groups: the intellectual Schlegels, who are of German descent, and the middle-class business family—the Wilcoxes. In spite of the opposition between their views and interests, both groups depend on money: inherited money in the case of the Schlegels and money coming from successful business ventures in the case of the Wilcoxes. This is how the cultured Margaret Schlegel puts it:

'I'm tired of these rich people who pretend to be poor, and think it shows a nice mind to ignore the piles of money that keep their feet above the waves. I stand each year on six hundred pounds, and Helen upon the same, and Tibby will stand upon eight, and as fast as our pounds crumble away into the

sea they are renewed—from the sea, yes, from the sea. And all
our thoughts are the thoughts of six-hundred-pounders . . .'

We are told of Mr. Wilcox:

'The genial, attentive host disappeared, and they saw instead
the man who had carved money out of Greece and Africa, and
bought forests from natives for a few bottles of gin.'

There is a pleasant period flavour about the novel where the
characters use the slang of 1910, where a man is a 'rotter' or
a 'cur', where the car is referred to as 'the motor', but in
spite of its material stability there is already a hint of doom in
the constant references to the menace of Germany, and more
subtly in the hints of cracks appearing in the spiritual fabric of
society. The first hint comes in a description of the withdrawn, wraith-like Mrs. Wilcox, who is the owner of
Howards End and stands midway between the two groups:

'She was sitting up in bed, writing letters on an invalid table
that spanned her knees. A breakfast tray was on another table
beside her. The light of the fire, the light from the window,
and the light of a candle-lamp, which threw a halo round her
hands, combined to create a strange atmosphere of dissolution.'

The 'strange atmosphere of dissolution' is the crux of the
matter. This world is on the brink of collapse because its
values are inadequate. Its primary value is the cult of personal relationships:

'. . . personal relations [we are told] are the important thing
for ever and ever, and not the outer life of telegrams and anger.'

But 'personal relations' are of their nature fragile. We are
told in another place:

'She . . . had seen the reliable walls of youth collapse. Panic and emptiness! Panic and emptiness!'

For they do not rest on any firmly held system of beliefs. The religion described in the book is 'genteel' like the characters. This is Margaret Schlegel meditating on an English Christmas:

'[She] felt the grotesque impact of the unseen upon the seen, and saw issuing from a forgotten manger at Bethlehem this torrent of coins and toys. Vulgarity reigned.'

It is the vulgarity and the materialism which offend her, not the 'forgotten manger at Bethlehem.'

'She was not a Christian in the accepted sense [we read]; she did not believe that God had ever worked among us as a young artisan.'

The central symbol is the house called Howards End. This is how the novelist describes it:

'In these English farms, if anywhere, one might see life steadily and see it whole, group in one vision its transitoriness and its eternal youth, connect—connect without bitterness until all men are brothers.'

The house stands for something real and deeply appreciated, but also for something that is threatened, that is growing faint. The crucial word is 'connect', and it recurs throughout the novel. All these people are trying, with an underlying desperation, to 'connect'. Margaret Schlegel is contrasted with her eccentric sister Helen. Her motto is 'connect' and she marries the widowed Henry Wilcox, the man who had 'bought forests from natives for a few bottles of gin,' because she feels that the Wilcoxes 'keep England going', and because she hopes that a connection between what she and they stand for may somehow save the situation:

> 'Now she never forgot anyone for whom she had once cared; she connected, though the connection might be bitter, and she hoped that some day Henry would do the same.'
> ' "One isolates", said Helen slowly . . .' And because "one isolates" there is no solution. "Life", concludes Margaret, "is being melted down, all over the world." '

Although in some ways a less enjoyable book than *Howards End*, *A Passage to India* is a finer achievement. It was, as we know, published fourteen years later. During these fourteen years the process of 'melting down' had proceeded apace, and the issues appear far more starkly and far more tragically against the Indian background. This is the opening paragraph:

> 'The very wood seems made of mud, the inhabitants of mud moving, so monotonous is everything that meets the eye, that when the Ganges comes down it might be expected to wash the excrescence back into the soil. Houses fall, people are drowned and left rotting, but the general outline of the town persists, swelling here, shrinking there, like some low but indestructible form of life.'

It is an extraordinary vision of disintegration: people reduced to the spectacle of 'mud moving', to 'excrescence', 'left rotting'. Only the 'outline of the town persists' with humanity transformed into 'some low but indestructible form of life'.

With Mr. Forster, as with other contemporary writers, we find 'moments of vision'—moments in which the characters suddenly recognise that something irrevocable has happened to them; moments in which not the meaning but the essential meaninglessness of life becomes apparent to them. The opening glimpse of the collapse of humanity leads directly to the central moment in the Malabar caves:

'. . . the echo began, in some indescribable way, to undermine her hold on life. Coming at a moment when she chanced to be fatigued, it had managed to murmur, "Pathos, piety, courage—they exist, but are identical, and so is filth. Everything exists, nothing has value". If one had spoken vileness in that place, or quoted lofty poetry, the result would have been the same—"ouboum".'

The passage speaks for itself. It is the logical outcome of the description of Mrs. Wilcox in bed. What was there no more than a hint, a suggestion of 'a strange atmosphere of dissolution', has turned into the dissolution of the values on which the old world rested:

'Pathos, piety, courage—they exist, but are identical, and so is filth. Everything exists, nothing has value.'

Virginia Woolf belonged to the same generation as Mr. Forster, and the same set. She was a less distinguished novelist than he and though she possessed some of his virtues, her books are even more symptomatic than his of the predicament that I have been trying to describe. Her first two novels, *The Voyage Out* and *Night and Day*, were published in 1915 and 1919. They were traditional in form and it was not until the appearance of *Jacob's Room* in 1922 that she attempted a full-length novel in the experimental style which was to make her famous. The new style was not the result of sudden inspiration. It was foreshadowed in some critical essays which appeared two or three years before *Jacob's Room*. In the famous essay called 'How it Strikes a Contemporary' we find her praising Scott and Wordsworth for their belief in life.

'In both [she wrote] there is the same natural conviction that life is of a certain quality. They have their judgement of conduct. They know the relations of human beings towards each other and towards the universe. Neither of them probably has a word to say about the matter outright, but everything depends on it. Only believe, we find ourselves saying, and all the rest will come of itself.'

In another essay written about the same time, and called 'Modern Fiction', we find her writing in these terms of contemporary novelists:

'Look within and life, it seems, is very far from being "like this". Examine for a moment an ordinary mind on an ordinary day. The mind receives a myriad impressions—trivial, fantastic, evanescent, or engraved with the sharpness of steel. From all sides they come, an incessant shower of innumerable atoms; and as they fall, as they shape themselves into the life of Monday or Tuesday, the accent falls differently from of old; the moment of importance came not here but there . . . Life is not a series of gig lamps symmetrically arranged; life is a luminous halo, a semi-transparent envelope surrounding us from the beginning of consciousness to the end. Is it not the task of the novelist to convey this varying, this unknown and uncircumscribed spirit, whatever aberration or complexity it may display, with as little mixture of the alien and the external as possible?'

There are several things to be said about these passages. Mrs. Woolf tried, in her novels, to do two things which turned out to be incompatible. She wanted to preserve the conviction, the belief, that life is of a certain quality, which she found in Scott and Wordsworth and which was ultimately traceable to the fact that they were living in a society which still accepted certain fundamental religious beliefs. She also wanted to include certain aspects of experience which found no place either in those writers or in the work of her contemporaries.

The second passage is not simply a criticism of contemporary fiction in general. It was part of an onslaught on Bennett, Wells and Galsworthy whom she stigmatised as 'materialists' and who all owed, directly or indirectly, a good deal to the French Naturalists. What is of particular interest, however, is that in this second passage she herself appears as the heir—rather remote, a trifle pallid and very belated—but nevertheless the heir of the French Symbolists. Huysmans, who began as a disciple of Zola, was making a similar criticism in *Là-bas* when he attacked the Master's brand of Naturalism and entered a plea for what he called 'un naturalisme spiritualiste'. Laforgue and Rimbaud did not speak in very different terms of the alexandrine that they were throwing overboard. Nor were their aims very different from Mrs. Woolf's. She, too, was trying to capture 'the moment that never returns', was trying to find a way out of the materialist prison. Her art has the same novelty as theirs, but there are serious weaknesses which are foreshadowed in the vagueness of phrases like 'luminous halo', 'semi-transparent envelope', and 'unknown and uncircumscribed spirit'. They are equally apparent when she tries to catch the moment of vision, or probe the deeper layers of experience:

'. . . the great revelation perhaps never did come. Instead, there were little daily miracles, illuminations, matches struck unexpectedly in the dark.'

Plainly, the mystery, the revelation or whatever it is meant to be, is *not* there. All that is there are words: 'miracles', 'illuminations', the trite 'matches struck unexpectedly in the dark'.

One at least of the reasons why her novels are lacking in the conviction and stability that she admired in the great writers of the past can be seen in her handling of Miss Kilman in *Mrs. Dalloway*:

> 'Also she did a little Extension Lecturing and so on. Then Our Lord had come to her (and here she always bowed her head). She had seen the light two years and three months ago. Now she did not envy women like Clarissa Dalloway: she pitied them.'

The spectacle of religious fanaticism is not a pleasant one. Yet Miss Kilman raises issues with which the novelist is not competent to deal, but which she feels cannot be ignored. Miss Kilman strikes a discordant note in the polite world because, in spite of her ignorance and fanaticism, she is a challenge to its fundamental complacency. She is a symbol of violent, subterranean feelings which threaten to break through the delicate technique. This is evident in the fumbled descriptions of her. Mrs. Woolf takes refuge in a facile, self-protective irony. Miss Kilman is represented as a figure of fun: poor, ugly, awkward, she 'stood on the landing, and wore a mackintosh; but had her reasons'.

Virginia Woolf's career as a novelist ended differently from Mr. Forster's. After *A Passage to India* he wrote no more novels: after *To the Lighthouse* the disintegration which threatened the world of fiction actually invaded the novels themselves. There are no longer characters in any serious sense: there are wraiths and voices.

Lawrence's background was working class and Nonconformist. Mr. Forster and Mrs. Woolf were the product of nineteenth-century liberal agnosticism. Yet in spite of their differences, they had certain things in common. They all record the destruction of a world. There was a good deal of the prophet in Lawrence. He recorded the collapse of the old world and the advent of the machine age. But he tried to find a way out of the human predicament. He protested against the de-humanisation of man. He tried, as we have seen, to discover a new mode of consciousness, a new way of life. We know the result. It is a picture of frustration and disillusionment. Mr. Forster and Mrs. Woolf were content to record the disappearance of the old order. They offered no positive programme, no 'message' of hope. Mr. Forster once protested that the age suffered from too much faith. He went on to boast that his faith was spelt with a small instead of a capital letter. And the fundamental weakness of his work, as of Mrs. Woolf's, is a lack of faith. They believe, in a general way, in personal relationships and tolerance and freedom, but they are without any clear conception of the Good Life. People must be kind and sensitive and tolerant and free. Then, somehow or other, all will be well. That is all. And because they lacked any strongly held positive beliefs and spelt their faith with a small letter, their world fell to pieces.

It may seem a far cry from these writers to the world of 'the absurd' of the Existentialists, or the sub-human world of the American 'tough' school like Hemingway and Henry

Miller, but in reality it is not. Civilised values often survive for a time the beliefs which created them, but only for a time. In the end the elegant superstructure collapses. When the world of Mr. Forster and Mrs. Woolf fell into ruin, man did indeed find himself in a world which was meaningless, which appeared 'absurd'. It is the same with their characters. What all their characters have in common, whether they are 'tough guys' or sensitive souls, is that they are examples of what Edwin Muir called 'the Natural Man' as opposed to 'the Christian Man'. Even if the belief is implicit, these writers do believe that man has no resources outside himself. Those who seem to be looking for moments of vision are looking for a secularised vision. That is the great difference between the Impressionist and the Baroque artists. In the seventeenth century the supreme moment—the moment of ecstasy or of death—was religious: in the work of the Impressionists 'the moment that never returns' is secularised; it is a matter of changing light coupled with changing physical reactions in the artist who himself is no more than 'a bundle of perceptions' or, as Laforgue put it, a 'keyboard on which nature plays in a certain way'.

I have said that one of the functions of the supernatural is to conserve the natural, that when it is absent the natural withers and dies. Perhaps 'degenerates' would be a better word. 'The Natural Man' is completely conditioned by heredity and environment as Zola so clearly saw. It is Pascal's equation minus the 'angel'. The civility of the characters of Forster is only skin deep. They can very easily turn into the sub-men—the barely articulate sub-men—of Hemingway who are reduced to the sum of their animal instincts: hatred, lust and greed; or to Henry Miller's herd of rutting animals.

They may equally well find their niche in the Party like the characters in Malraux's *Condition humaine*, or again become the robots of Samuel Beckett's plays: the tramps waiting in vain for Godot; the blind tyrant and the limbless imbeciles immured in dustbins in *Fin de partie*. For the 'end game' is also the end of man.

III

PROBLEMS OF BELIEF

CLAUDEL—MAURIAC—GREENE

III

In chapter one I said something about the difficulties of a Christian writer which spring directly from the fact that in modern times he belongs to a minority culture. There are, broadly speaking, two possible approaches open to him. He may adopt a radically Christian standpoint, disregard (in so far as he can) the changes which have taken place during the past four hundred years, and write resolutely against the grain of his age. Alternatively, he can accept the situation in which he finds himself and try to give a Christian interpretation of the modern world.

In this third chapter I am going to examine in some detail the work of three contemporary Catholic writers: two Frenchmen and one Englishman; two novelists and one poet. They are Paul Claudel, François Mauriac and Graham Greene. Claudel adopted the first of the two alternatives I have just mentioned; Mauriac and Greene the second. It has been said of Claudel that he is outside the modern crisis and therefore remote from our present anxieties; it has been said of the other two that, instead of interpreting the modern age in the light of Christian belief, they have pushed compromise to the point at which it becomes *complicity*. I propose to consider the truth of these criticisms.

There are certain French poets who present a special problem for Anglo-Saxon audiences. Corneille and Racine are the most celebrated examples, but we meet the same problem in Victor Hugo and Claudel. It is the problem of language. It is not that the French they wrote is particularly difficult; it is the difficulty of accustoming ourselves to poetry which is very unlike English poetry, to poetry which seems abstract, rhetorical, declamatory. Racine now has a small band of devoted admirers in these islands and hostility to Corneille is diminishing, but it has taken three hundred years. It is possible that the same thing may happen with Claudel, whose drama has aroused little enthusiasm in England or America.

In the case of Claudel the problem of language is complicated by the personality of the man which pervades every line he wrote. There can be no doubt that he was the most formidable personality in the European literature of the first half of the twentieth century. It is from this fact that any attempt to assess his achievement must start.

'I am not a *bel esprit* [he once said in a letter to Jacques Rivière]; I am a simple, serious man. As an artist I despise virtuosi, and I do not understand practical jokers. The sneer, from Voltaire to Anatole France, has always seemed to me to be the sign of the damned. As soon as a man is possessed by the hatred of God, he is unable to prevent himself from laughing.'

The simplicity, the solemnity and the intolerance of these sentences bring home to us the rugged power of the man which left its mark on his contemporaries.

'It is no good thinking that we can bring to Claudel a cold admiration! [said the young Jacques Rivière in a letter to the young Alain-Fournier]. It is not our taste that he cares about pleasing; he demands our soul so that he can offer it to God. He wants to force our innermost consent. He is determined, in spite of ourselves, to wrench us from doubt and dilettantism.'

It was this determination to impose himself, to force peoples' 'innermost consent', which either frightened or impressed his unbelieving contemporaries, and which produced the drama of his relations with Gide.

'As a young man [Gide wrote in his diary in 1905], Claudel looked like a nail; now he looks like a sledgehammer. Not a very high forehead, but rather wide; face without subtlety as though carved with a chisel; bull neck continued by the straight line of the head, through which passion can rush and flood the brain . . . He gives me the impression of a solidified cyclone. When he talks, it seems as though something were released inside him; he proceeds by a series of sudden assertions and maintains a hostile tone even if you agree with him.'

Another entry made twenty years later shows that time had not weakened the impression:

'In the presence of Claudel, I am conscious of what I lack; he dominates me; he oppresses me; he has more base and surface, more health, money, genius, power, children, faith etc. than I have. I only think of piping down.'

The correspondence between Claudel and Gide was much more than an exchange between two famous writers; it was a dialogue between the two poles of the French intelligence; a clash between the mobile, sceptical mind of a Montaigne or a Pascal, and the earthy, conservative, orthodox mind—the mind of a Bossuet or of Claudel himself. Certain phrases stand out: phrases which throw considerable light on this particular representative of the Christian tradition: 'sledgehammer', 'solidified cyclone', 'dominates me'. For the granite-like faith, which was so different from the restless

51

questioning of a Mauriac or a Greene, the power and fanaticism of the man dominated everybody who came into contact with him, forced their respect even when they withheld their 'innermost consent'.

I have used the word 'intolerance'. It is inescapable when discussing Claudel. His intolerance frightened his opponents, but it was the main cause of his failure as an apologist when dealing with a man like Gide. It also led to astonishing errors in his judgements of writers.

Claudel's hostility to the writers of the Enlightenment is understandable. He lived through the worst days of the spoliation of the Church in France at the hands of the anti-clericals whom he regarded as the heirs of Voltaire and Diderot. It did not stop there. He refused to allow any virtue to writers who were known to have held anti-clerical views, or whose good faith he suspected. When a literary journal invited him, in common with other eminent men of letters, to send a message for the tercentenary of Descartes' *Discours de la méthode*, he replied, acidly, that he had re-read the book and could see nothing in it. He hated Stendhal; he had no use for Flaubert; Zola was 'that disgusting Zola'. He admired Gide's work with reservations while he thought that there was a chance of making an important convert, but as soon as the fish slipped through the net Claudel discovered that his books were worthless. 'From an artistic and intellectual point of view,' he said in a notorious interview in 1947, 'Gide is nothing.'

'I know that we are only fair to people whom we like', he said at the end of one of his diatribes. There was usually something in what he said, but he went too far in his denunciation of famous unbelievers as he went too far in his indulgence for minor performers whose orthodoxy was beyond doubt.

Coventry Patmore emerged as a great religious poet, and it was thanks to Claudel's enthusiasm that G. K. Chesterton made a surprising and somewhat incongruous appearance in the pages of the *Nouvelle Revue Française*.

While Claudel's letters and essays may outlast his poetry, it is on his poetic dramas and on the poems contained in the *Five Great Odes* and *Cantata for Three Voices* that his reputation as a writer at present rests. In one of the essays in *Positions et propositions* he asserted that just as there is a perennial philosophy, so there is a perennial poetry which takes its themes from the created world in the manner of the liturgy. Claudel set out to write a perennial poetry which was to deal with eternal themes, which was to be a hymn of praise to a God-given universe. In his plays he chooses a critical moment in the spiritual evolution of mankind, but his procedure is the reverse of T. S. Eliot's. The setting is not a country house or a cocktail party. It is always far removed from contemporary civilisation either in time or space. It is medieval France or Renaissance Europe, the Napoleonic era or the time of the Vatican Council, the Caucasus or, most characteristic of all, a ship in mid-ocean.

The theme of the principal plays is the fortunes of the human couple in love. Claudel's conception of love clearly owes something to the 'fatal passion' of the Tristan legend, but the handling is Christian. His lovers are predestined for one another, but they are always separated by an obstacle which may be either moral, psychological or physical. Prouhèze or Ysé in *Partage de midi* has married the 'wrong man'; Sygne de Coûfontaine gives up her cousin and marries the appalling Turelure in order to save the Pope; Violaine contracts leprosy. Violaine and Sygne are saintly figures, but with

Ysé and Mesa, Prouhèze and Rodrigue, love becomes in fact or intention, adulterous. This of course is in keeping with the Tristan legend, but Claudel's aim is to show that good may come through sin, or that sin may be the means of finding God.

Love in Claudel, as surely as in the legend, is of its nature unhappy; but there is one serious flaw in the plays which has disturbed even Catholic critics. We have the impression that the lovers are unhappy because God intends them to be un-happy, that God is engaged in a cat-and-mouse game with his creatures, dashing the cup from their lips at the very moment when the obstacles to happiness and a Christian life have been removed. There is something repellent about the arguments of the priest who persuades Sygne to sacrifice herself and abandon her widowed cousin; and though Ysé's husband is dead, the curtain falls (as the stage direction has it) 'with a crash of thunder' as the house in which she and Mesa are hiding is blown to pieces. Whether they are saints or sinners, violent death following violent passion is the fate of nearly all these people. It is impossible to avoid the feeling not merely that Claudel's God has more in common with the tribal god of the Old Testament than with the Christian God of the New, but that He resembles the poet himself in one of his harsher moods.

Claudel described *The Satin Slipper* as a résumé of all his work. It is regarded by many of his critics as his most impor-tant play: it is certainly his most ambitious. It is part poetic drama and part farce, part morality play and part fantasy. It opens in sixteenth-century Spain, but the setting expands to embrace Europe, Africa, America, Asia, the whole world. It is one of the most striking productions of our time, but if it exemplifies Claudel's characteristic virtues it also exemplifies his most serious weaknesses. There is little genuine dramatic tension; the characters are abstractions engaged in propagating the poet's ideas; and the exaggerated symbolism gives it an air of unreality. The source of these weaknesses is to be found in some words spoken by the hero:

> 'It is not in order to become in my turn silence and immobility that I have broken a continent in two and crossed two seas. It is because I am a Catholic; it is in order that every part of humanity may be re-united.'

The plain fact is that it is much more a work of propaganda than a work of art. Claudel tried to create a Catholic world-conqueror and show him adding continents to the Church, but not even his eloquence could breathe life into this phantom; and the parallel between Rodrigue, who is stripped of his honours and sold as a slave, and Our Lord seems frankly grotesque.

Before I leave Claudel's plays I want to draw attention to the curious contrast between *The Satin Slipper* and *L'Annonce faite à Marie*. *The Satin Slipper* is an example of the way in which Claudel writes against the grain of the age and tries to produce a work of absolute Christian art in an age of declining religious belief. He was no doubt trying to do the same thing in *L'Annonce faite à Marie*, but in that play, which seems to me to be his most impressive achievement, the artist got the better of the propagandist. Our sympathies are clearly supposed to be with Violaine: the saintly woman who contracts leprosy, who is forced to abandon home and fiancé and live in a hovel, and who miraculously brings back to life the child of her sinful younger sister who has married her fiancé. Now

55

whatever the poet's overt intention, his real sympathies (as surely as in a novel of Mauriac's) are with the sinner. Mara steals the play. That is why, when I saw a stage performance of it a few years ago in France, I came away with the impression that it was indeed an achievement, but would have been even better if Mauriac had been able to revise it, or had collaborated with the formidable dramatist!

In the remarkable account of his conversion, Claudel pays tribute to the importance of the part played by Rimbaud in his spiritual development by showing him a way out of the materialist prison of the nineteenth century. But Rimbaud was also one of the major influences in his literary development. Claudel has explained his verse technique in a long essay in *Positions et propositions*. I cannot discuss in any detail the complicated theory of stresses and pauses, or the importance he attached to the arrangement of words on the printed page, but there are one or two things which must be said. Claudel introduced a personal form of what I am tempted to call 'free verse'. His own word was *verset*, which is the French term for a verse of the Bible. It was formed by a study of the Bible, the liturgy, the prose poetry of Baudelaire's *Petits poèmes en prose*, Rimbaud's *Illuminations* and, to a lesser extent, the free verse of Walt Whitman. He needed flexibility and suppleness; he needed an instrument which though capable of the dignity and eloquence proper to poetry, remained close to the spoken word and was therefore suitable for drama. But he wanted something else besides. He wanted an instrument which though possessing the flexibility of the free verse of the Symbolists, would also possess the weight, the drive, the declamatory qualities of the alexandrine as used by the great French dramatists of the seventeenth century. That is the crucial point. The regularity and uniformity of the alexandrine were organic; they were a reflection of a certain stability and order which belonged to the age that had brought the alexandrine to perfection. That order finally came to an end in the nineteenth century when the alexandrine fell into partial disuse and was replaced by *vers libre* or *vers libéré*. In other words, Claudel wanted it both ways. While taking advantage of the metrical freedom won by the nineteenth century, he was trying to restore unity, or the appearance of unity, by *force*.

Let us look now at a sample of his non-dramatic poetry:

> Hail then, O world new to my eyes, O world that is
>   now total!
> O creed entire of visible and invisible things,
>   I accept you with a catholic heart!
> Whichever way I turn my head
> I behold the immense octave of Creation!
> The world opens and, however wide the span,
>   my eye traverses it from end to end.
> I have weighed the sun like a fat sheep that two strong
>   men suspend on a pole between their shoulders.

This passage from the second of the *Five Great Odes* is a fair illustration of the strength and weakness of the non-dramatic poetry. We can hardly fail to be impressed by the loftiness of the voice, the marked liturgical movement, or the grandeur of the vision with its emphasis on words like 'total', 'entire', 'span' and 'octave of Creation', its conception of the hierarchy of being from God down to the 'fat sheep'. Once again, however, the crucial word is the word 'catholic'. Claudel clearly intended it in the double sense of 'Christian' and 'universal'; but his poetry is always at the service of religion, and for me 'catholic', in its present context, is a word of limitation. Claudel does not forge new concepts out of theological terms as Eliot does in the *Four Quartets*: he uses them as a means of appealing to the beliefs of his readers in a manner which is both different from and less impressive than Eliot's. This is symptomatic of all his work. It means that his poetry is not creative in the full sense, that it does not possess either the intensity or the precision of the greatest poetry.

I think we must go on to conclude that what was wrong with Claudel was a curious defect of intelligence. He was, as his fanaticism shows all too clearly, a man in whom powerful emotions were not matched by a correspondingly powerful intelligence—the intelligence we find in a high degree in Eliot—which enables a writer to re-think traditional concepts, to sift and test his experience, and finally to introduce a fresh pattern which alters our ways of thinking and feeling.

In *God and Mammon* François Mauriac speaks enviously of converts like Maritain and Péguy for whom Catholicism was a free choice. 'My own drama', he writes, 'lies in the fact that I was born into it; I did not choose it; this religion was imposed on me at birth.'

These words illustrate very clearly the difference between medieval and modern, between a religious and a secularist society. Religion is not regarded as a bond between the individual and the community, but as something 'imposed' on him which tends to isolate him from the communal life. Baptism no longer means for him the entry into a Christian society; it is a mark which sets the Christian apart from society as a whole.

Mauriac's point of view is made clearer in another famous passage:

'I am a metaphysician who works in the concrete. Thanks to a certain gift of atmosphere, I try to make perceptible, tangible and odorous the Catholic universe of evil. I make incarnate that sinner of whom the theologians give us an abstract idea.'

In Mauriac's novels religion is 'the destructive element'. It is the source not of harmony, but of conflict, or rather a series of conflicts: the conflict between the Church and the world; between the love of God and the love of the creature; between the individual and his environment; the individual and his family; the individual and the community.

In his most successful novels the basic situation is always the same. It is the predicament of a person caught in a trap. It is the trap formed by the smug landed gentry, by the family, by a de-spiritualised provincial society.

All Mauriac's critics have remarked on his special tenderness for the sinner. Now Mauriac sees the sinner as essentially the victim of his environment. The sinner is the man of passion who is driven into rebellion by his environment. He rebels against middle-class complacency, and rejects religion simply because it is the religion of the middle classes whom he cannot abide.

Mauriac is fond of quoting Kierkegaard's dictum that the contrary of sin is not virtue but faith. There is only one sin in his world that really counts. It is the sin of apostasy. The main conflict in the novels is between two different passions, between two different loves. There is an unbridgeable gulf between the property owners and the sinners: there is no comparable gulf between saints and sinners. For saints and sinners are men of passion like Mauriac himself; the only difference between them is their choice of object and the quality of their love. The sinner rebels against middle-class complacency and is drawn, without realising it, in the direction of the saint but is diverted from his goal by temptation. It is, indeed, his horror of middle-class complacency which drives him to rebellion, but also into sin and crime, into preferring the creature to the Creator before he can find the right path. It is his wanderings and not the attainment of his goal which provide the Catholic novelist with his subject.

The 'outsider' and the 'prisoner' are two of the most significant figures to be found in modern fiction. The 'outsider', the man who does not fit into contemporary society and ends by disrupting it, has had a long and successful run since Stendhal invented him; and no one has expressed more powerfully than Proust the terrors of a man trapped in a psychological prison. Mauriac's particular contribution is to have shown that the 'outsider' and the 'prisoner' are, or may be, complementary aspects of the same personality.

It is because they do not fit in and because they are a threat to the sacred family that characters like Thérèse Desqueyroux and Louis, the protagonist of *Nœud de vipères*, feel that they are trapped, that they are prisoners with the family circle watching them, preparing to close in on them. The psychological pressure of the family circle and the feeling that escape is physically and psychologically impossible produces the climax. It drives them to the Act of Violence, to the attempt to break out of the 'trap', which turns the 'outsider' into the sinner who is the counterpart in the order of Grace of the outsiders of a Stendhal, a Gide or a Camus in the order of nature.

It also gives the novels their violence: a violence which extends to incident, imagery and vocabulary. One of the characters in *Nœud de vipères* speaks of 'the reasonable and moderate religion which has always been held in honour in our family'. That is not how his unbelieving father sees it.

'I pretended to take it for an authentic representation of Christianity', he says, 'in order to have the right to hate it.'

It is an observation of capital importance to which I shall return.

A good deal has been written about Mauriac's complicity with his sinners. The truth is that he uses them as a protest against a society which is fundamentally unchristian. They are rebels against a society which he himself detests, but from which he cannot escape, which in fact has provided him with his opportunities by making it possible for him to write books without having to worry about earning a living.

Mauriac has a good deal in common with Graham Greene. I want to glance at one of two of the principal works of the English novelist before I try to draw some general conclusions. The setting of most of Mauriac's novels is the desolate *landes* where men live in small, isolated, ingrowing groups. The setting of Greene's novels is sometimes a secularised suburban community, but also the wilds of Mexico, the desolate Gold Coast, or Indo-China where his characters are both physically and spiritually exiles. In his most satisfactory novels he adapts the technique of the adventure story to his purposes. Mauriac's 'outsider' is matched by his 'hunted man': Pinky, the juvenile delinquent in *Brighton Rock*, the whisky priest in *The Power and the Glory*, the police officer corroded by a curiously sentimental form of pity who is spied on and psychologically pursued in *The Heart of the Matter*. He dwells perpetually on the squalor of his characters' surroundings. 'Shabby', 'dusty', 'sour', 'rotting' are recurrent words. Both *The Power and the Glory* and *The Heart of the Matter* are punctuated by the sound of vultures flapping their wings or beating their wings on corrugated-iron roofs; *The Heart of the Matter* by the continual sight of rats and cockroaches. If *The Power and the Glory* is the best of Greene's novels, it is because the whisky priest on the run in Mexico is a valid symbol of a certain aspect of contemporary life.

Where both novelists are most open to criticism is the poor view that they take of human nature and the quality of their religion as it is exhibited in their work. Mauriac's work is heavily coloured by his Jansenist outlook. What is most important about Jansenism from the critic's point of view is that it does approximate to the Protestant attitude towards the Fall of Man, to the belief that Original Sin led to the complete ruin of human nature which is incapable of any good action without the direct intervention of Grace. The protagonists of practically all Mauriac's novels are spiritually and emotionally bankrupt. I have already quoted the passage in which Louis speaks of accepting the religion of his family as an authentic representation of Christianity in order that he should have 'the right to hate it'. His characters seek not the good qualities of their fellow men, but their bad qualities in order to have the right to hate—the right to unleash the most destructive feeling known to erring human nature, to that feeling which at once opens the door to all the other deadly sins.

We find the same sad, twisted religion in Greene: this is how he speaks of the protagonist of *The Heart of the Matter*:

'He had always been prepared to accept the responsibility for his actions, and he had always been half aware too, from the time he made his terrible private vow that she should be happy, how far *this* action might carry him. Despair is the price

62

one pays for setting oneself an impossible aim. It is, one is told, the unforgivable sin, but it is a sin the corrupt or evil man never practises. He always has hope. He never reaches the freezing point of knowing absolute failure. Only the man of good will carries always in his heart this capacity for damnation.'

While we can say of Mauriac that his novels are the projection of something unbalanced in his view of human nature, Greene's seem to me to raise a much more serious question. It seems to me that there is an element in his novels which can only be described as *abnormal*. In *Brighton Rock* Pinky broods over what the novelist calls 'the frightening weekly exercise of his parents which he watched from his single bed'. In the same novel 'Phil opened an eye—yellow with sexual effort'. Again: 'You could know everything in the world and yet if you were ignorant of that one dirty scramble you knew nothing.'

Mauriac's preoccupation with sexual relations verges on obsession, but though his accounts of them are coloured by an extraordinary feeling of guilt, there is a no less powerful sense of delight—delight in the forbidden thing. Yet it is very different from Greene's attitude. The 'single bed' is a sign of a morbid shrinking from natural processes; the 'yellow' and the 'dirty scramble' go beyond morbid isolation: they reveal a view of human nature which is warped to the point of abnormality.

What is common to all three writers whom I have discussed here is the element of *violence*. Claudel really did strive for an integral Catholicism, but it led him not merely to set most of his plays in a period remote from our own, but to try to *impose* religion on his experience, to restore by force a link between the individual and society which in the ages of faith had been natural and organic. Mauriac and Greene seem to me to go to the opposite extreme: their religion is essentially the sort of religion we find when the pattern is imposed by the age, when man moulds his religion instead of himself being moulded by it.

That is not the whole story. While literature is bound to be coloured to some extent by the age, while we cannot expect to find the serene untroubled vision of a Dante in an age of secularism, we still have to ask why violence has become peculiarly a characteristic of Catholic writers during the past hundred years. The explanation seems to me to lie in the inferiority of the writers' religious to their artistic experience. A Christian is obliged to conform to a rigid code, to accept certain restraints. The tension that this creates is increased when he is living in a society in which the majority of people are indifferent or hostile to religion. It is increased still further when the Christian happens to be an imaginative writer living at a greater pitch of intensity than the common run of men. The disparity between the quality of his religious and his artistic experience means that religion fails to provide a proper discipline, that the depth of his artistic experience is not balanced by a corresponding depth of religious experience. This leads to overcompensation through violence. Instead of seeking a discipline, he seeks an outlet and uses his writing as a safety valve.

Mauriac seems to me to be in much the same position as his own trapped characters: the novels are symbolical Acts of Violence which give the illusion of escape from the trap. Once again we have to note a difference between Mauriac and Greene. Mauriac's characters are fornicators, adulterers, even murderers; they hate their fellows. But neither fornication, adultery nor murder has quite the same horror as some of Greene's endings: the gramophone record in *Brighton Rock*, the suicide in *The Heart of the Matter*, or the cremation of the saint in *The End of the Affair*. The crimes of Mauriac's characters are appalling: they are not and never have been abnormal.

I am going to make a comparison. It is a comparison which may sound rather unfair, but it enables me to bring out an important point. I am going to compare the work of the novelists I have been talking about with what is by common consent one of the greatest novels ever written. In one of those long discourses on religion in *The Brothers Karamazov*, Ivan Karamazov speaks disparagingly of God creating the world 'according to the geometry of Euclid'. He speaks again of possessing a 'Euclidian earthly mind', of 'the impotent and infinitely small Euclidian mind of man', and of his own 'pitiful, earthly, Euclidian understanding'. Although 'Euclidian' is not, perhaps, the right word to describe the effect on us of the world of Mauriac or Greene, they do somehow give us an impression of constriction. I think it can be expressed by saying that their outlook is theological rather than religious. There is a certain lack of spontaneity. We feel that they have been browsing too much over theological treatises without always understanding them; that everything is somehow too cut and dried; that men are either black or white, that they react according to an obvious mechanism, so that the conversion of the sinner can nearly always be foreseen. A work like Bernanos's *Diary of a Country Priest* is in many respects a most excellent novel, but it has two very evident weaknesses. In the first place it is really only intelligible to an instructed

65

Catholic. In the next place, we never get inside the skin of the country priest because the novelist has tried to do something which is plainly impossible: he has tried to describe the experience of a saint from the inside.

Now let us look at a passage from *The Brothers Karamazov*. The speaker is Mitya:

'Beauty is a terrible and awful thing! It is terrible because it has not been fathomed and never can be fathomed, for God sets us nothing but riddles. Here the boundaries meet and all contradictions exist side by side. I am not a cultivated man, brother, but I've thought a lot about this. It's terrible what mysteries there are! Too many riddles weigh men down on earth. We must solve them as we can, and try to keep a dry skin in the water. Beauty! I can't endure the thought that a man of lofty mind and heart begins with the ideal of the Madonna and ends with the ideal of Sodom. What's still more awful is that a man with the ideal of Sodom in his soul does not renounce the ideal of the Madonna, and his heart may be on fire with that ideal, genuinely on fire, just as in his days of youth and innocence . . . What to the mind is shameful is beauty and nothing else to the heart. Is there beauty in Sodom? Believe me, that for the immense mass of mankind beauty is found in Sodom.'

Virginia Woolf speaks in one of her essays of Dostoevsky's characters giving the impression that they have lost their clothes in some terrible catastrophe. To the western reader there certainly seems to be an element of lunacy in the Dostoevsky world, a love of extremes which appears, superficially, to be very similar to the love of extremes and the violence that we find in Catholic novelists. We must, however, distinguish. What is astonishing about the passage I have just quoted is the extraordinary insight into the complexity of human nature. It is not at all a question of black or white, but of the two. The conflict is a real one. There is no possible doubt about the reality of those 'riddles', or about the simultaneous tug of wildly conflicting ideals—the ideals of Sodom and the Madonna. It has been said of Dostoevsky, as we are bound to say of Mauriac and Greene, that his sinners and his villains are much more convincing than his saints. Once again we must distinguish. Ivan is plainly the most exciting character in *The Brothers Karamazov*, but it is misleading to suggest that Alyosha has anything in common with Mauriac's rather pallid saints. He is plainly an essential component in the novel who counterbalances the ravings and extravagances of his two brothers. But Dostoevsky was too great a novelist to try to show us Alyosha from within. What he does is to concentrate on his effect on other people: his extraordinary authority, the attraction he exercises over them, and finally the way in which he contrives to soothe the maddest of them. For, as Mgr. Romano Guardini so justly observes, in his relations with other people a sort of greatness becomes apparent. And that greatness is the greatness of sanctity.

The situation that I have described to you in these lectures is a curious one. Writers reject the view that belief is a hindrance to them and have nearly always gone out of their way to find some philosophy or system which will provide, or so they hope, a framework for their experience, which will enable them—to borrow a distinction of Santayana's— to achieve 'wholeness' as well as 'fulness'. Their experiments are by no means always happy. The philosophy often has a bad effect on their art, or alternatively when their books succeed, they seem to succeed in spite and not because of the particular philosophy or system they have adopted. This has applied with particular force to those writers who have been practising Christians. Some writers like James Joyce have left the Church and signalled their departure by an excellent novel : others have entered it and announced their arrival by a thoroughly bad book, or have ceased to write at all. Are we then to conclude that the unbeliever is right, that though literature unsupported by definite beliefs tends to be, admittedly, imperfect, it is nevertheless less bad than a literature imbued with the Christian faith ? I do not think that this is so. In an introduction written some years ago to a translation of Barbey d'Aurevilly's *Les Diaboliques*—a work which incidentally exemplifies most of the weaknesses I have been discussing—Mr. Peter Quennell spoke in these terms :

> 'Catholic writers have this great advantage—that, since they are conscious of the tremendous moral implications of an isolated word or gesture, their vision of life has a heightened quality, an intense dramatic relief, which is often beyond the reach of the matter-of-fact agnostic, whose standards, though possibly more rational, from a literary point of view are sometimes far less stimulating. Everything counts—nothing is trivial or insignificant—in Barbey's curious universe; and it is his art to bring out the dramatic intensity, the moral light and shade, of every subject that he touches on.'

The work of Claudel, Mauriac, Greene and many other writers who wear the uncomfortable title of 'Catholic poet' or 'Catholic novelist' does indeed seem to me to be very imperfect. But in spite of 'yellow' eyes, 'dirty scrambles', in

spite of an inadequate realisation of the complexity and contradictions of human nature such as we find in Mauriac and
Greene, in spite of theological muddles and Catholic suicides,
at least these writers are serious. Their characters behave
appallingly; they are not simply a prey to all the vices, they
introduce fresh horrors which only people who had mulled
over the text-books of the theologians—particularly the
moral theologians—could possibly have thought of, but they
do not reduce humanity to a 'temperament', an 'appetite', to
a bundle of instincts or, as I said earlier, to a herd of rutting
animals like the characters in a novel by Henry Miller. They
do remind us on every page that human beings, however vile,
have immortal souls; that the alternatives salvation-damna-
tion are the greatest reality, indeed the only reality, in the
world.

W9-ADP-284

David Cariens

The America We All Want

Protecting Your Community from Gun Violence

HighTide
Publications, Inc.

High Tide Publications, Inc.
1000 Bland Point Road
Deltaville, Virginia 23043
www.HighTidePublications.com

Ordering Information: Quantity sales. Special discounts are available on quantity purchases by corporations, associations, and others. For details, contact the "Special Sales Department" at the address above.

Printed in the United States of America

ISBN: 978-0692705971

Table of Contents

Acknowledgements   i
Introduction   ii
Precis   v

Part 1 What happened to my country?
Chapter 1   Sins of the Fathers   1
Chapter 2   The Killings Multiply   11
Chapter 3   Actually, Guns Do Kill   25

Part 2 If you tell a lie long enough, it becomes the truth.
Chapter 4   The Second Amendment   31
Chapter 5   No Silver Bullet   39
Chapter 6   Shell Games And Lies   51

Part 3 Investigations without integrity are worthless
Chapter 7   More Corrupt Than I Thought   65
Chapter 8   How Much Is Your Child Worth?   79
Chapter 9   No Value For Life   89
Chapter 10   What Will It Take?   99

Part 4 Taking control in our communities
Chapter 11   What Parents Can Do   109
Chapter 12   Think Local And State.   119
Chapter 13   Creative Approaches   127

Index   139

About the Author   145

Acknowledgements

This book would not have been possible without the support given me by many friends and family members. In the fourteen years since Angela Dales, the mother of my oldest grandchild was gunned down at the Appalachian School of Law, I have had to come to terms with the reality few people in positions of authority want to face up to, much less do anything about, the slaughter in our schools, movie theaters, offices, homes, and a wide variety of public venues.

First and foremost, I owe a special debt of gratitude to Janice Cariens for her excellent editing of this book and her suggestions for improvements.

Second, to Jeanne and Carl Johansen, your encouragement and support for all my writings on gun violence have meant a great deal, as have your ideas and suggestions about content. You two have been the best tonic a writer could have; I can only say a very deep, and sincere "thank you so much."

Third, I would like to add a word of thanks to the members of the *Rappatomac Writers* and *Chesapeake Bay Writers* who have been a continual source of support. They are a great group of talented people who have encouraged me at every turn to keep writing and to try to do something—through words—to end the carnage.

Fourth, to Lancaster County Virginia Sheriff Patrick McCranie, his deputy, Bill Webb, and Northumberland County Sheriff James R. "Doc" Lyons, a very special thanks. These three men took time out of their busy schedules to talk with me about community policing, their outreach programs, and concerns for the lives of the men and women in their respective departments.

And fifth, to the people I have met along the way at book signings and talks, while I don't remember all your names, I do remember your kind words and encouraging me to keep writing on this important subject.. Thank you very much; your thoughtfulness means a great deal to me.

David Cariens

Kilmarnock, Virginia – August 24, 2016

Introduction

Nearly fourteen years have passed since the shooting at the Appalachian School of Law. In those years, approximately 31 school shootings in the U.S., resulted in the deaths of 126 people and the wounding of another 98.

Angela Dales, the mother of my oldest grandchild, was killed at the Appalachian School of Law shooting. Danny Dales, Angie's father, died in January 2013. His health deteriorated sharply after his daughter's death and he never recovered. Her mother, Sue, has moved to be near her son and his family. Our granddaughter has graduated from college with honors and is headed to graduate school. Our son no longer blames himself for not being in the student lounge to protect Angie. His recovery from Angie's murder was long and costly. It took a good six years of support and thousands of dollars in medical bills to get him back on his feet. Our scars will never heal.

Virginia has not done nearly enough to make our schools safer since the shooting on January 16, 2002. Virginia had the worst school shooting in this nation's history: April 16, 2007, Virginia Tech 32 dead and at least 17 wounded. The parallels between the state's two shootings are staggering: ignored warning signs, failed leadership on the part of school leaders on the day of the shootings, massive cover-ups, and in the case of the Virginia Tech rampage, illegal actions on the part of the Virginia Supreme Court concerning who was in charge of the investigation. Sadly, gross incompetence has been covered up, and the gun show loopholes have not been closed. This has opened the door to people who are a danger to themselves and others and made it easier to buy a gun in Virginia.

In the case of the Virginia Tech shooting, the state spent over $675,000 to have a company who relies on the state for some of its income, write the analysis of the shooting to determine if the state's largest university was culpable. This was an obvious conflict of interest and waste of taxpayers' money. In contrast, both the Columbine report was written at no cost by the panel who did the investigation. The report analyzing the tragedy at Sandy Hook was written by the state's Attorney General's office at no extra cost to the taxpayers.

In Virginia, the state hired two public relations organizations to slant the point of view of the tragedy in order to do minimal damage to Virginia Tech. The firms, *Firestorm* and *Burson-Marsteller,* were paid a total of $813,000. Neither Colorado nor Connecticut needed to hire public relations firms to manage the media because they had nothing to hide.

In Virginia, the lies persist.

Precis

The America We All Want is the culmination of over a decade of research and writing on gun violence in the United States. The book draws on research as well as the author's extensive writings including his books on the shooting at the Appalachian School of Law and Virginia Tech. The author brings to the problem more than 50 years of working in intelligence and crime analysis. He also has the added dimension of having lost a family member in a school shooting.

The book is brutally honest in addressing the causes of the gun violence epidemic in the United States. The author asserts past failures of our national and state leaders to address the root causes of violence are, in large part, why this country faces public shootings on a scale not known before.

But the book does not stop there. The author factors in the growth of terrorism, racially motivated violence, and the horrendous targeting and murder of our police.

The America We All Want suggests action to take at the local level to curb these shooting rampages. The book does not have all the answers, but is a clarion call for people to think about what can be done and then follow up with actions. The author rejects the premise that changing the system is impossible because it is corrupt.

This book challenges those who when presented with ideas to curb the gun violence say, "This won't work," or " That won't work," to come up with their own ideas for curbing gun violence. It also challenges readers to work at the local level for change; to attend town hall or council meetings and put forth ideas to stop the killings. And most important listen to each other's ideas. If you are conservative, listen to progressives; if you are progressive, listen to conservatives. This book summons readers to think about gun violence: to listen to others, to learn, and to act.

The underlying message of the author's words is, if you are one of those who only complain and criticize, then at least have the decency to get out the way of people who are trying to stop the blood baths in our schools, theaters, shopping malls, and on this nation's streets.

Finally, the author asserts the road to curbing gun violence will be long, painful, and many innocent people will lose their lives because of our past failures to act. We need to take action now.

The situation is serious, but not hopeless.

The America
We All Want

Part 1

What happened to my
country?

Chapter 1

Sins of the Fathers

You do not have to be Albert Einstein to know this country faces one of the most complicated, complex, and serious challenges to its safety and survival since our founding in the late 18th Century—gun violence.

The men who have led this country over the last five or six decades have failed us miserably. And I say men because they have, until recently, almost exclusively held the reigns of power in government and private business. Republican, Democrat, Tea Party, they all have fallen woefully short in formulating domestic policies to help keep us safe.

Our elected officials and our captains of industry joined in an unholy alliance to pursue self-centered, get rich policies at the expense of the good of the general public. Their actions have undercut our national interests, undermined public safety, and decimated the middle class. Government leaders and private business joined forces in an ideological crusade to eliminate unions, maximize profits, ship jobs overseas, and as a result not only has our economy been damaged, but our safety and national security have suffered. Is it any wonder an atmosphere of anxiety and uncertainty among the populace is so prevalent?

At the time, all these leaders masquerade as patriots.

Are They Loyal To Anyone Other Than Themselves?

Our business and political leaders have demonstrated a stunning ignorance of world affairs and lack of even the most rudimentary knowledge of other cultures, not to mention being oblivious to the threats we face both from within our country and abroad.

Nowhere is this failure more apparent than in the dramatic rise of gun violence in this country. Catastrophic failures in domestic and foreign polies have come home to roost.

There is no one single source of this violence. The shooters may be self-radicalized Americans; disturbed individuals who want to lash out at innocent people in schools, theaters, nightclubs, or shopping malls; or adherents to terrorist ideologies and ideas. The problem is not simple; the solutions will not be easy.

To begin, citizens are being mowed down in record numbers at a rate never before seen. Americans have to recognize there is a multiplicity of complex causes and there is no one quick fix, answer, or solution.

Add to the above, the shootings of innocent, law-abiding African Americans in poor areas of our cities. And now, the slaughter of police and firemen, the people we rely on for our safety. We are paying for the sins of those who were in power for decades; men who lacked imagination, initiative, and backbone.

In many respects we are a country making no effort to engage in logical, sound thought or reasoning..

The picture is grim, but not hopeless.

Roots of the Evil

In the absence of a Congress ready to act to reduce gun violence, we will keep working to create a different Congress.

Gabrielle Giffords

Some of this gun violence has its roots in both disturbed, home-grown individuals who are seeking to revenge imagined injustices against them, and some are inspired by DAISH* (ISIL) or other terrorist groups.

In other cases several motives come together with catastrophic results such as Orlando, where an individual was apparently self-radicalized while struggling with his sexual orientation, fell prey to DAISH propaganda. (I will discuss the lone wolf and foreign terror threats in the next chapter.)

Couple the preceding with people who are hell bent on accumulating vast amounts of wealth no matter the cost to our national treasure, reputation, and most importantly, the lives of young Americans, and you have a recipe for the complete unraveling of our society.

Factors such as foreign-inspired terrorism; the failure to provide widespread and accessible mental health care; unstable citizens unfettered access to rapid-fire military-style weapons, hatred of innocent people with alternative life styles; paranoia about the security and future of this country; anxiety about people's financial future; and the failure of people in positions of trust and authority to find solutions to even our most rudimentary economic and political problems, have come together in a horrendous and destructive assault on this nation's wellbeing.

In the past, we had the luxury of two oceans to separate us from the turmoil in Europe and Asia; we had friendly neighbors to the north and south. Now, the oceans no longer isolate us, and the long (and at times isolated) borders with Canada to the north and Mexico to the south, are opportunities for our enemies to exploit.

---

*I use DAISH because it has a slightly pejorative tone to it taking away some of ISIL's credibility because it does not give them the status of being a state.

Incompetent Leaders

In the more than eight decades since World War II, the United States has put bandages on problems, allowed the profit motive to cloud clear thinking, allowed our health care system to deteriorate in the hands of greedy insurance companies and private health care providers, failed to implement widespread and easy access mental health care, and the unsuccessful use of force to solve what Washington perceived as threats from overseas.

The most striking examples of our failed policies are the Vietnam War and the invasion of Iraq. Indeed, the latter has opened a conflict for which we are not prepared. Since the invasion of Iraq, the U.S. has found itself in a struggle the likes of which it has not seen before— terrorism on a worldwide scale.

The problem with the ill-conceived Iraq adventure will take decades to solve, cost thousands of lives, and divert badly needed funds from our schools and the rebuilding of our infrastructure. The invasion of Iraq has brought violence to our homeland.

In the past our nation deceived itself into thinking we were rich enough to buy our way through any problem or crisis. And indeed in the first couple of decades after the fall of Nazi Germany and Imperial Japan there seemed to be some truth in this approach, e.g. the Marshall Plan in Europe and our rebuilding of Japan.

But, as a nation, we became lazy. More and more, the people we elected to office were ill prepared to hold office and failed to understand international problems much less societies based on different value systems. They viewed everything through a rosy, unrealistic American prism thinking everyone wanted to be just like us in every way.

Before the Iraq invasion, the propaganda fed to the American public was, *we will be welcome*. Instead, before too long they greeted us with Improvised Explosive Devices (IEDs).

Now, we are engaged in the longest war in this nation's history. Between 2003 and 2011, 4,497 young Americans have lost their lives in Iraq and another 2,356 were killed in Afghanistan. In addition, some 32,222 were wounded, psychologically or physically in Iraq and 18,675 in Afghanistan.

The great minds in Washington failed to examine how someone like Saddam Hussein could be ousted from within. They failed to play devil's advocate and ask, "Is there another way to oust this monster without spending trillions of dollars, killing thousands, and wounding many more thousands?"

Our elected officials turned to people who told them what they wanted to hear. They did not turn to substantive specialists. An intelligence analyst, who was involved in the preparation for the invasion of Iraq, told me, "They (the Bush Administration and some members of the Intelligence Community) fell in love with the idea of war. They were naïve and victims of their own shoddy research and analysis."

Washington failed to recognize that while Saddam Hussein was a tyrant, he was Iraq's tyrant and not one superimposed by the U.S. military. It never occurred to the great minds in our nation's capital that invading a country, no matter how noble the intentions, resulted in the invaders becoming occupiers and, after a few months, hated ones.

We have no one but ourselves to blame for the crisis; the ill-conceived policies of the first decade of this century have brought us to where we are today.

Gentlemen: We Need To Fix It

Approximately 97% of mass murderers are males; they invariably signal their intent to commit violence through a variety of traits: most notably, their problems with women.

The Orlando killer, Omar Mateen, beat his first wife and a friend quoted him as saying he "hated women because you have to be nice to them to get sex." Seung Sui Cho stalked and harassed women at Virginia Tech before he went on his rampage; Peter Odighizwa, the killer at the Appalachian School of Law, was also a wife beater and at one point took control of a class, ranting about the evils of women; and Isla Vista, California murderer Elliot Roger, threw things at women who did not pay attention to him and lamented he was still a virgin and had never even kissed a girl.

How many more examples of threatening traits are needed before we take action to keep guns out of the hands of these mentally disturbed people?

How about starting with laws prohibiting men who stalk, harass, or beat women from owning any gun at all. And let's not stop there. Any man who drags an unconscious woman behind a dumpster and rapes her, is an out-of-control low-life who should never be allowed to own a weapon. (The case of Brock Turner, a 20 year old Stanford student who on January 18, 2015 dragged an unconscious female behind a dumpster and attempted to rape her.)

Does it ever occur to these sick men who these women are: our mothers, sisters, daughters, wives, and aunts: the women we love.

Gentlemen you can do something about these shootings. Your manhood is not measured by the size of your gun; it is measured by the size of your backbone and your willingness to speak up and demand laws to put an end to this violence.

A Convergence Of Evils

The United States is faced with a convergence of evils: terrorism, hatred of people with non-traditional life styles, untreated mental illness, decades of feckless political leaders at the state and federal levels, business executives who sell the safety of our schools as well as the nation's intelligence and security apparatus for 30 pieces of silver, and the availability of military-style weapons to anyone without doing a background check or even asking the buyer why he or she wants the gun.

There is no simple solution to ending the gun violence. It is a complex problem. We are faced with threats requiring thought and well-reasoned responses. Our patience combined with thoughtful action is necessary if we are to rid ourselves of the slaughter in schools, nightclubs, theaters, shopping malls, and on our streets.

The picture is not hopeless, but it is serious. Progress has been made in curbing gun violence, but it has been at the local level, not the federal or in some cases the state level.

Together we will examine this crisis in greater detail in the following chapters and look at what is being done at the local level and what has to be done.

The road ahead will be long, the battles hard fought, and more lives will be lost, but we need to begin acting now. This gun violence crisis is largely of our own making and is not going to end until we act.

Chapter 2

The Killings Multiply

Lone Wolf Killings

Lone Wolf killers are not a new phenomenon. They have been around for decades even though we may not have called them Lone Wolves.

Remember Charles Joseph Whitman, an engineering student at the University of Texas in Austin? On August 1, 1966 he took handguns, rifles, and a shotgun to the observation tower on the 28th floor of the university's main building. Over approximately a 90-minute period he gunned down 49 people, killing 16 of them. He was a Lone Wolf.

What is new is the increasing number frequency of Lone Wolf attacks on a broad spectrum of our society. As the attacks have increased, so have the motivations. Indeed, it is not uncommon for the perpetrator of a Lone Wolf-style assault to be motivated by multiple reasons. The Orlando nightclub killer, Omar Mateen, is a case in point; an apparent self-radicalized Muslim American he also was struggling with his own sexual orientation. The latter resulted in his lashing out at the LBGT community. On June 12, 2016, he carried out the worst mass shooting in this nation's history, killing 49 people and wounding another 50.

Intelligence and crime analysts most often define Lone Wolf as an individual terrorist taking action without a leader or hierarchy. Another definition is a person who with or without foreign direction furthers his or her political or social goals through violence in violation of federal or state criminal law. Still others define Lone Wolf more broadly as anyone who lashes out, kills or maims whether it is for the sake of killing or because of an ideology. Whether you define Lone Wolf in narrow or broad terms, it is clear, Lone Wolf killings are on the rise.

Key Factors

Two trends in the United States have converged with horrific consequences—our no-questions-asked, easy access to guns and the sharp decline in mental health care. Then add to the mix the potent lobbying of the National Rifle Association, whose advocacy for unfettered access to guns is tantamount to defending the rights of those who are a threat to themselves and others, and you have the recipe for mass shootings.

We are a nation who prides itself in the rights granted to all of us by the Constitution. It also appears we are a nation where everyone has rights, but few have responsibilities.

We are a nation in need of a major overhaul of our psyche. All of us have to rethink the balance between our individual rights and our collective security. When mass killings occur you rarely, if ever, hear about the rights of those who have been gunned down. What you hear is our right to bear arms.

There is an emotional lack of logic tied to our Second Amendment rights to own and bear arms. You can talk calmly and rationally to most Americans about almost all of the Bill of Rights; you can debate where our rights of freedom of speech begin and where they end. But with many, you cannot talk logically about the right to bear arms; you cannot raise with them the fact that advocating uncontrolled access to guns is tantamount to defending the rights of mass killers such as Adam Lanza, Seung Hui Cho, and Peter Odighizuwa to own guns. Many Americans do not think the problem through. They do not recognize or admit democracies such as Canada, the United Kingdom, and Australia, all put limits on gun ownership, specifically rapid fire, military-style weapons.

Until there is a major reset of the American psyche, there will be no peace. Pending this shift in consciousness there will be no way to appreciably cut back on mass shootings.

No matter what category the self-radicalized killers fall into, they exhibit signs of, or are, mentally ill. Prime examples of this are psychopaths such as Eric Harris who apparently had a messianic superiority complex, and Seung Hui Cho who suffered from selective mutism, an anxiety disorder.

Small Cell Extremists

Then there was the Beltway sniper—a form of Lone Wolf attacks only with two men rather than one. In October 2002, John Allen Muhammad, aged 42, and Lee Boyd Malvo, 17, killed ten people and wounded three others in a serious of random Lone Wolf-style, sniper attacks in the Washington, D.C. metropolitan area. Muhammad's killings had a paralyzing, psychological impact on the nation's capital, bringing the city to a near standstill.

The Lone Wolf: Not Just An American Phenomenon.

On July 22, 2011, Anders Behring Breivik, motivated by extremist causes including anti-multiculturalism, anti-Islam, anti-government, and anti-immigration beliefs, killed 76 people and wounded another 100.

Breivik, a paranoid schizophrenic, began his campaign of terror by bombing a government building. Then, a few hours later, he boarded a ferry to Utoya Island posing as a policeman. The island is the site of a Workers' Youth League Camp. Once there he opened fire intermittently for an hour slaughtering 69 people.

Victims of Our Success

In the case of Whitman and Muhammad, guns were the weapons; in the case of Brivik, he used bombs and guns. Lone Wolves, then, are not limited in their choice of weapons.

Our success against DAISH (ISIL) in Iraq and Syria, where terrorist organizations have steadily lost territory over the last few years, has, ironically forced them to turn to Lone Wolf style attacks in the U.S., Europe, and elsewhere.

In a highly sophisticated use of the Internet and mass media, DAISH, has succeeded in radicalizing young people who have no idea about the true nature of the organization. They appear to be drawn to the mystic of fighting for a cause, fighting for the underdog. Some are troubled individuals who want to join with DAISH and become a Lone Wolf, as a way to get redress for the real or imagined injustices of society. Others apparently are misfits or are individuals with deep psychological problems surfacing in a desire to kill and hurt innocent people.

Whatever the motivation, we now face a Lone Wolf threat arising from multiple causes, a Lone Wolf crisis the likes of which we have not seen before.

Police Lives Matter

Police lives matter, they have always mattered. The warning signs have been blinking red for quite a while, but people in positions of authority looked the other way. It was only a matter of time until members of law enforcement became targets of Lone Wolf killers.

According to the National Law Enforcement Memorial Fund, 1,439 officers have died in the last ten years in the line of duty, an average of 1 death every 61 hours. The Memorial Fund also reports there were 15,725 assaults on officers in 2015, resulting in 13,824 injuries, and 123 deaths. Violence against police officers is such an everyday occurrence and many of these deaths often go virtually unnoticed—a headline today, forgotten tomorrow.

We trust the police to keep us safe, but we do not give them the salaries they deserve. We put our lives in their hands and don't think enough of them to provide adequately for their children's education if they are killed in the line of duty.

Local police are building bridges to minority communities in an effort to improve community-police relations and build trust and understanding.

Where I live in eastern Virginia local sheriffs are taking the initiative and reaching out to county residents. *The Northumberland County Virginia Sheriff's Department* works closely with a Citizens' Advisory Panel and is actively involved in the local *Boys and Girls Club*s.

To tackle problems and complaints from one community in the county, the Lancaster County Sheriff's Department hosted a cookout aimed at establishing rapport, understanding and trust between residents and the police. As a result of these outreach programs there has been a significant improvement in police-community relations and the number of complaints against the police have dropped significantly.

Lancaster County also has a *Shop With A Cop* program. At the beginning of each school year ensuring children have the school supplies they need. The program has existed for seven years and has helped hundreds of children. *Shop With A Cop* is funded by churches, civic organizations, and individual Lancaster Country residents.

In neighboring Northumberland County Virginia, the story is much the same. The Sheriff meets regularly with local organizations and clubs to help improve community relations. In August 2016 alone he had six such meetings with local citizens' groups.

Indeed, the sheriffs of both Northumberland and Lancaster counties have made community policing a high priority and they are getting results. Both Virginia Sheriffs want everyone treated fairly; they want everyone—police and local residents—to go home safely to their families every night.

A few bad policemen across the country have led to widespread negative misconceptions about law enforcement officers. And in many people's minds, unfortunately, perception becomes their reality. The truth is the vast majority of our police, and our firefighters, are highly dedicated individuals we can trust and point to with pride.

Dallas

The deadliest attack on law enforcement was 9/11 when 72 officers died responding to the terrorist attack. The second deadliest attack on law enforcement officers occurred this year. On July 7, 2016, Lone Wolf Micah Xavier Johnson shot and killed five police officers in Dallas, Texas and wounded another nine. Johnson also wounded two civilians in his killing spree.

The shooting occurred at the end of a *Black Lives Matter* peaceful protest. Johnson, an Army Reverse and Afghan War veteran, was upset over the killing of Alton Sterling in Baton Rouge, Louisiana and Philando Castile in Falcon Heights, Minnesota.

A standoff followed the massacre and the following day Johnson was killed by a bomb attached to a remote control bomb disposal robot.

The following officers were killed in Dallas:

- Brent Thompson, 43, a Dallas transit police officer.

- Patrick Zamarripa, 32, a Dallas police officer who served three tours in Iraq in the U.S. military.

- Michael Krol, 40, who joined the Dallas police in 2008.

- Lorne Ahrens, 48, a former semi-pro football player and 14-year veteran of the police force.

- Michael Smith, 55, the father of two and long time veteran of the department.

Johnson used an antique Eastern European rifle designed in the 1940s and imported in great numbers to the U.S. It is a semi-automatic weapon and does not use a detachable magazine. It holds 10 rounds of ammunition.

Then Baton Rouge

The Dallas tragedy was followed a few days later by another atrocity. Lone Wolf Gavin Long, a Kansas City man and former Marine who had served in Iraq, drove to Dallas and then on to Baton Rouge where he opened fire on Sunday morning, July 10, 2016 killing three police officers and wounding three others.

The officers killed were:

- Montrell Jackson, age 32. Jackson was a ten-year veteran of the police force and leaves behind a wife and infant.

- Brad Garafola, age 41. He had been with the police department less than a year.

- Matthew Gerald, age 45. Gerald was deputy with the East Baton Rouge Sheriff's Office. He was the father of four.

Long used an AR-15 military assault rifle; it can be bought in many states with no questions asked.

Money—Part Of The Problem

Our states, towns, and counties back away from funding training for their police. As a result many, through no fault of their own, are not prepared for what they face. An alarming few have active shooter training and many are not given community interaction courses. And perhaps worst of all, some police departments are so underfunded they cannot do background searches on new officers.

This later point played a roll in the tragic death of 12-year old Tamir Rice in Cleveland, when Timothy Laehmann, was hired by the Cleveland Police Department without a background check. The officer had been let go by a suburban police department having been deemed emotionally unfit for service. (I discuss the Tamir Rice tragedy in detail in the next section of this chapter.)

We have come to the point where not only are the police used for target practice, but our firefighters as well. Schools, colleges, and universities; their professors, instructors, and teachers, have become targets. The epidemic spreads.

Black Lives Matter

Black Lives Matter is not racist; it is a statement of fact.

When we turn our law enforcement responsibilities over to amateur, armed Neighborhood Watch posses, whose racism is bolstered by Stand Your Ground laws, what do you expect?

Whatever Travon Martin's crime, and I am not sure he committed any crime, was his killing justified? Did the punishment fit the crime? No.

The Killing of 12-Year-Old Tamir Rice

On November 22, 2014, two Cleveland city police officers, 26-year-old Timothy Loehmann and 46-year-old Frank Garmback, responded to a report stating a black male was sitting on a swing pointing a gun at people. The caller, at the beginning of the call and in the middle, said, "It's probably fake." The caller also said, "he is probably a juvenile." This information was apparently not relayed to the two police officers.

When the two officers arrived, the 12-year-old black male pointed the gun at them. Within two seconds, Loehmann fired two shots into Rice, killing him.

Neither officer attempted to administer first aid to the wounded youngster.

Officer Loehmann had resigned from the Independence, Ohio police force (a suburb of Cleveland) rather than face termination because of concerns over his fitness as a police officer—concerns over his emotional stability. An Independence police memorandum asserted Loehmann was unable to follow "basic functions as instructed," and cited a "dangerous loss of composure." The document also indicated his handling of weapons was "dismal" and he became visibly "distracted and weepy" because of an unspecified personal relationship.

According to media coverage of the tragedy, the Cleveland Police Department never bothered to do a background check on Loehmann, or look at the file on him. On December 28, 2015, a Grand Jury returned their decision declining to indict the police officers.

On April 25, 2016, the City of Cleveland agreed to pay Tamir Rice's family $6 million.

It's Not Just Tamir Rice

There are many sad, unfortunate killings of African-Americans:

- Michael Brown age 18, August 9, 2014 shot and killed in Ferguson, Missouri;

- Eric Garner age 43, July 17, 2014, illegally choked in New York;

- Rumain Briston 34, December 2, 2014, who was shot and killed by a Phoenix police officer who mistook a pill bottle for a weapon;

- Walter Scott 50, April 4, 2015, who was shot and killed by a police officer while running away from a traffic stop for a broken taillight.

The Common Good

Given the rate at which bodies are piling up, it appears many Americans seem to find violence deeply satisfying. Our elected leaders at the national level have shown themselves to be useless when it comes to ending the gun violence. Leaders from the left and right appear to be blind to the carnage and deaf to the cries to stop the violence; they excel at bloviating and seem to have an obsession with hot air. They have no moral compass and few, if any, appear to believe in doing anything for the common good. Many of our national leaders have a deliberate indifference when it comes to ending shooting rampages and finding ways to reduce violence.

If we are to have change, clearly it will have to begin as a grass roots movement. It is up to each one of us to take action when and where we can, and to make our voices heard. When you see or hear someone advocating violence take action and get the person help.

When you see someone expressing an interest in obtaining, and using weapons and explosives, or bomb-making manuals to use in violent actions—report him or her.

If you see or hear someone expressing a desire to attack a person or physical target, report him or her. The same can be said for those who express solidarity and or admiration for lone wolf extremists or killers, report him or her to authorities. The best FBI leads come from walk-ins. I will return to what you can do to prevent gun violence in the following chapters.

Chapter 3

Actually, Guns Do Kill

For over fourteen years I have analyzed and written about mass shootings; for over fourteen years I have seen little done to end the slaughter.

Mass slaughter on school grounds, in theaters, in churches, and in shopping malls may be the most serious and complex problem in this nation's history. Solving the problem will take careful and deliberate thought, but thinking is hard work and there are no easy solutions. Those few who do propose ways to reduce the epidemic of gun violence are met with a fusillade of emotions on why their ideas won't work.

The Violence Grows

Since January 16, 2002, when Angela Dales, the mother of my oldest grandchild, was gunned down at the Appalachian School of Law, the number of school shootings has steadily grown. The press reports there have been two school shootings a month in 2015, and as I am writing in late 2015-early 2016, there have been six more school shootings this month (February 2016) alone.

Since January 16, 2002, the bodies have continued to pile up: Virginia Tech, 32 killed and 17 wounded; Isla Vista, California, 6 killed, 13 wounded; Sandy Hook Elementary, 20 children and 6 teachers killed; and Umpqua Community College, Roseburg, Oregon, 9 killed,

7 wounded; and Orlando, Florida, 49 killed, 53 wounded. The people who were killed and wounded were shot, they were not stabbed; they were not beaten. Guns were used to kill and maim.

The far right of the American political spectrum says, "Guns don't kill, people kill." This is a no-brainer play-on-words. Cars don't kill either, but they can and do in the hands of people. Therefore, we license cars and their drivers. If a gun did not kill my family member then what did? The answer is a person *with a gun* killed Angela Dales.

Perhaps the most sobering statistic is there are, on average, 92 gun deaths a day in the U.S. We claim to be the greatest nation on Earth, but we do next to nothing when children are slaughtered at Sandy Hook Elementary School, or worshipers are massacred at a prayer service in Charleston, South Carolina, or a TV reporter and cameraman are murdered on live television in Roanoke, Virginia.

Frightening Statistics

The statistics are compelling and frightening. According to *Mother Jones*, "Between 1982 and 2011, a mass shooting occurred in the United States every 200 days. Between 2011 and 2014, a mass shooting occurred every 64 days." As the magazine points out, "The frequency of mass shootings has tripled since 2011."

On October 1, 2015 a 26-year-old white male killed eight people and wounded nine others at Umpqua Community College in Roseburg, Oregon. Just eight days later, on October 9th, there were two school shootings in one day. One person was killed and three were wounded at Northern Arizona University. Later in the day, one person was killed and one wounded at Texas Southern University.

The answer is not more guns. The United States has over 300 million guns in private hands, or nearly one gun for every citizen.

The answer is to find ways to keep guns out of the hands of those who are bent on mass public executions.

The America
We All Want

Part 2

If you tell a lie long enough, it
becomes the truth.

Chapter 4

The Second Amendment

A well-regulated Militia, being necessary to the security of a free State, the right of the people to keep and bear Arms, shall not be infringed.

Some claim there should be no restrictions on gun ownership; to restrict a person's right to buy and own a gun, in any way, violates the Second Amendment of the Constitution.

The Second Amendment was written in the late 1700s when this nation was being formed and there was a genuine fear the British would attack and try to return us to colonial status. This is the background to the reference to Militia up front in the amendment. I am not diminishing the current interpretation of the Second Amendment emphasizing citizens' rights. But I am urging the use of common sense when projecting the founding fathers' words forward two centuries without thinking.

When the Second Amendment was written, the standard weapon was a musket. It took time to load the musket ball, pour in the powder and fire one shot. I have fired one of those muskets, I know.

When I was a boy, my father and older brother used to take me to a quarry to fire my brother's 1862 civil war musket. It takes a long time to load and fire. Mass killings by one person with a musket were impossible in the 1700s.

The founding fathers did not imagine rapid-fire assault weapons. There were no six-chamber pistols, nor were there AK-47s. There were no multi-bullet magazines mowing down or wounding large numbers of people in just a few minutes. I find it hard to believe our founding fathers would sanction allowing those bent on harming others to have unfettered access to weapons capable of killing dozens of people in just a few seconds.

No one wants to take away or limit the rights of mentally sound, decent, law-abiding citizens to own a gun for protection, hunting, or target practice. Gun ownership and hunting are part of our heritage. It does give me pause when a person wants to own a rapid fire, repeating weapon. Why someone needs magazines to hold more than nine bullets is beyond me. Most, if not all of these weapons were developed for the military to kill enemy soldiers. These weapons were not meant for hunting, they were meant for killing people. They are being used to efficiently kill human beings in our schools, churches, theaters, shopping malls, and offices.

What I Want

What I want is to keep guns out of the hands of people who have been deemed a threat to themselves or others. We can dramatically reduce the numbers of school shootings and incidents of gun violence if we would keep weapons out of the hands of those people.

Misguided Second Amendment proponents come up with an endless list of reasons as to why various proposals are bad, or why a proposal violates individual rights. Second Amendment proponents are people you go to when you want to be told, "This or idea is no good" or " violates the Constitution." They have no ideas or counter proposals, all they have is criticism. The main staple of their vocabulary is "no." Even Jeb Bush, when asked to comment on the recent spate of school shootings, shrugged his shoulders and said, "Stuff happens."

We, as a nation, seem paralyzed to take action. Every time legislation is proposed that might help curb the epidemic of gun violence, Second Amendment advocates decry it as a violation of Constitutional rights to bear arms. Nowhere do they mention the Constitutional rights of the dead and wounded victims.

The problem of gun violence in this country has reach epidemic proportions and it is getting worse. From Columbine, to Grundy, to Blacksburg, to Aurora, to Charleston, to Roseburg, to Northern Arizona on it goes. The bodies are piled higher and higher, and we take no action to end the carnage.

No Easy Solutions

There is no easy solution. The causes are numerous: lack of mental health care, failure to recognize these shootings are a male-related crisis (as I noted earlier, 97% of the mass shootings are done by males), no universal background checks for people buying guns, and politicians who have sold out to gun manufacturers and the National Riffle Association (NRA).

The sharp rise in gun violence can be pinpointed to the states' cutting back mental health care services and facilities. In many instances people who are a threat to themselves or others have no place to go. In Virginia the mental health care system is dysfunctional. When state Senator Creigh Deeds tried to get his son committed for treatment, he was told there was no bed available. In fact beds were available. Within 24 hours of being denied treatment, Deed's son seriously wounded his father and then killed himself.

Despite the promises in Richmond to allocate more resources to mental health following the Virginia Tech rampage, the state spends less on mental health care today than it did on the eve of April 16, 2007—the Virginia Tech rampage.

There are no cheap fixes to the problem of gun violence, but one thing is clear, letting a student kill others is an abdication of responsibility and authority.

Time And Money

It will take time and money—lots of both to stop and reverse the increasing number of mass shootings. It will take mandatory background checks to keep guns out of the hands of those who are a threat to themselves and others as well as terrorists, domestic abusers, and convicted felons. Nowhere in the Constitution does it say any of these groups have a right to own and keep firearms.

Since the shooting at Virginia Tech on April 16, 2007, approximately 142 have been killed or wounded on school grounds in the U.S. And those figures only scratch the surface of the total number of gun-related deaths in this country. The slaughter goes on.

Innocent people are mowed down in places of learning and houses of prayer; we wring our hands, cry, and pray. Our legislators cut funds for mental heath care despite the unanimous opinion of mental health care experts affirming a broader approach to mental health care would reduce all crimes.

Other Nations

Other nations have adopted effective measures to stop the public slaughters. Following a mass shooting in 1996 when 35 people were killed and 18 wounded, Australia adopted a series of measures resulting in significant, positive results. Canberra, the capital of Australia, rallied behind a widespread gun buy-back campaign and enacted strict gun laws.

The net result of Australia's actions has led to a marked decline in suicides and murders with guns. Since 1996, Australia has had only one mass shooting.

According to the Library of Congress Law Library, "Great Britain has some of the most stringent gun control laws in the world. The main law is from the late 1960s, but it was amended to restrict gun ownership further in the latter part of the twentieth century in response to massacres involving lawfully licensed weapons. Handguns are prohibited weapons and require special permission. Firearms and shotguns require a certificate from the police for ownership, and a number of criteria must be met, including the requirement an applicant has a good reason to possess the requested weapon. Self-defense or a simple wish to possess a weapon is not considered a good reason. The secure storage of weapons is also a factor when licenses are granted."

Great Britain has a well-deserved reputation of having some of the tightest gun control laws in the world. Again, the Library of Congress Law Library notes, "Only police officers, members of the armed forces, or individuals with written permission from the Home Secretary may lawfully own a handgun. This stringent legislation may, in part, account for Britain's relatively low statistics for the use of firearms in crime—in 2008–2009 firearms were used in only 0.3% of all recorded crimes and were responsible for the deaths of thirty-nine people. ..."

"Firearms laws governing the country (Great Britain) have generally been enacted in a reactive manner in response to massacres and overwhelming public support backing the introduction of prohibitions on firearms. The laws cover a number of weapons, including handguns, shotguns, imitation firearms, deactivated firearms, and air weapons..."

With these strict gun laws, Great Britain remains a democracy where individual rights are guaranteed and protected. The absence of an armed citizenry has not led to a dictatorship.

The self-proclaimed greatest nation in the world does not sit idly by while those who are a threat to society use innocent people for target practice. The increase in mass shootings has shown it is crucial the people demand elected officials help stop the killings.

Chapter 5

No Silver Bullet

There are no quick fixes to solving the epidemic of gun violence in this nation. There is no silver bullet.

It will take years, even decades, as well as a great deal of money and dedication to tackle the multiplicity of causes feeding the epidemic of school shootings.

Not Enforcing Laws

Some Second Amendment advocates say we don't need new laws, we need to enforce the ones we have. There is some truth in their call for enforcing existing laws and regulations. While it is a good place to begin, it is only a small beginning. We not only need to strictly enforce existing laws, rules, and procedures, we need to hold people accountable for their actions and inactions when they fail to follow the laws on the books.

People in authority need to understand in dealing with threats of gun or other violence, erring on the side of caution is an imperative. Otherwise they will pay a price. If the message can get across, we can make a dent in the number of school shootings. But to do this, someone, at some time, must be held accountable for his or her actions or inactions. Time and time again, authorities have wasted valuable time when they did not act, resulting in lives lost and people hurt.

Signals

Most mass shooters send signals of their intentions. Shooting rampages are rarely spur of the moment or impulse crimes. In most cases, there are signals of impending violence. The killers, or prospective killers, are intelligent and cunning. Their crimes are carefully planned and carried out.

The killers often write a manifesto decrying the evils of society, or detailing the injustices they imagine they have suffered. For many of these mass murderers, their paranoia appears to know no bounds. Many want a moment of fame and glory, they are seeking to immortalize themselves through hideous crimes.

Researchers have found in a large number of school and mass murders there was the "Columbine effect." *Mother Jones* reports it "analyzed 72 plots and attacks in 30 states where suspects and perpetrators claimed to have been inspired by Columbine. Law enforcement stopped 51 before anyone was harmed. Twenty-one plots evolved into attacks, with a total of 89 people killed, 126 injured, with nine of the perpetrators committing suicide."

The magazine also reports "Individuals in 12 cases indicated their goal was to outdo the Columbine body count."

CNN reported in 2013 the FBI thwarted 148 mass shootings at high schools, up 33% from 2012. And even with the FBI's success, the body count grows.

Foiled Attack

A mass school shooting in Wascea, Minnesota was foiled on April 24, 2014 when a woman called 911 to report a young man apparently breaking into a storage unit. The young man was John LaDue, an

11th grader who was planning to carry out one of the worst, if not the worst, school shootings in this nation's history. Authorities found bomb-making equipment in the storage unit and in his school locker. The police also discovered LaDue's bedroom was an arsenal, two guns near his bed and five in a safe in his closet.

LaDue planned to start by killing his parents and his sister and then carry out a school shooting patterned on Columbine. Indeed, in the year before his arrest, he had become fascinated with the suburban Colorado school shooting, going so far as to buy a black duster jacket so he could dress like Eric Harris. LaDue also studied the Boston Marathon bombing and the Newtown, Connecticut massacre.

LaDue considered Adam Lanza a coward for killing first graders, but Dylon Klebold and Eric Harris were his heroes.

In September 2015, John LaDue pled guilty to a single felony count of illegal possession of an explosive. The press reported five felony counts of possessing incendiary devices were dropped in a plea deal to avoid prison. The young man will have to undergo up to 10 years of court-ordered treatment at a secure treatment facility for autism spectrum disorder in Atlanta, Georgia.

Warning Signs Ignored

Patterns of behavior are beginning to emerge. For example, I cannot find one instance of a female carrying out a mass school shooting in the United States. *Mother Jones* did find four instances where women were plotting mass shootings, but the police thwarted all four.

Given the overwhelming preponderance of male mass killers, we have to begin with the idea these killings are related to some sort of male crisis. Many of the killers had problems with women. Indeed, we see the genesis of the problem in many of these killers' relationships with or attitude toward women.

While the killers may not tell us when, where, and how the attack will take place, they do alert us.

Appalachian School of Law

In the case of Peter Odighizuwa, the killer at the Appalachian School of Law, he was a wife beater and in one classroom outburst pushed a professor from the podium and launched into an anti-female diatribe. He was banned from going into some school offices without an escort, and a student had to intervene to stop him from hitting the librarian because she was running the vacuum cleaner.

The warning signs were there. Some of the students had nicknamed him "the shooter." Three female faculty members were so concerned for their safety and the wellbeing of their students they asked for campus security. The law school had none. The school president brushed them aside saying, "You women and your hormones and your intuition … there is nothing to be afraid of, and it will be ok."

Within a few weeks Peter Odighizuwa went on a rampage and killed three people and wounded three others.

Neither the president of the Appalachian School of Law, nor any member of the administration was ever asked to explain the school's inaction when confronted with blatant acts of violence. And the school president was never called to task for ignoring faculty members' calls for school security.

Virginia Tech

Seung Hui Cho, who murdered 32 and wounded another 17 at Virginia Tech, harassed female students in person, over the phone, and via the Internet. He may have been frustrated because his advances toward females were rejected. Just days before his rampage, he went to Roanoke and hired a prostitute.

Just as in the case of the Appalachian School of Law, the killer's repeated warning signs were ignored.

Cho could have done little more to warn of his pending massacre than to put a neon sign announcing his intentions. Here are Cho's warning signs:

- October 15, 2005 Virginia Tech English Professor Nikki Giovanni wrote the head of the English department to report Cho's threatening classroom behavior. Giovanni wanted Cho removed from her class because she was concerned for her safety and the safety of her students. If the school did not remove him, she threatened to resign.

- In April 2006, Cho's technical writing professor, Carl Bean, suggested Cho drop his class. A heated argument ensued. During the spring of 2006, Cho's creative writing professor, Bob Hicok, expressed concern because Cho's writing was remarkable for violence.

- In the fall of 2006, Cho enrolled in a playwriting workshop taught by Professor Ed Falco. Cho wrote a play about a young man who hates the students at his school and planned to kill them and then commit suicide. The play was a blueprint for what happened.

- In September 2006, Professor Lisa Norris, another of Cho's writing professors, alerted Associate Dean Mary Ann Lewis to Cho's aberrant behavior. Professor Norris urged Cho to seek counseling.

Cho's harassment of women was well documented. On November 27, 2005, a female student complained about "annoying" Internet, phone, and in person contacts from Seung Hui Cho. On the November 30th, a second female student complained about Internet harassment from Cho.

A few days later, on December 6th, Cho continued his harassing ways and on the 6th, a third female student complained about unwanted, harassing messages and "disturbing" contacts from Seung Hui Cho. She filed a complaint and the school's police took action.

The Virginia Tech police notified Cho he was to have no further contact with the female student. A despondent Cho sent his suitemates an email saying, "I might as well kill myself now."

On December 13, 2005, after being interviewed by the police regarding the complaints against him, Seung Hui Cho sent emails to his dorm suitemates talking of suicide. They were alarmed and called the police. A screener at the police station evaluated him as "an imminent danger to himself and others." A magistrate issued a temporary detaining order and he was sent to Carilion St. Albans Psychiatric Hospital for mental evaluation.

Less than 24 hours after being ordered to the mental health facility, Seung Hui Cho, on December 14, 2005, was released from the Psychiatric Hospital after the staff psychiatrist, without extensive testing or gathering collateral information, ruled he was not a danger to himself or others. The hospital recommended Cho receive outpatient counseling.

Cho returned to Virginia Tech where he slipped under the radar until April 16, 2007, when he slaughtered 32 students and faculty and wounded another 17.

Isle of Vista

On May 23, 2014, 22-year-old Elliot Roger killed six people and wounded 14 in Isle of Vista, California. Roger's motive was revenge for sexual and social rejection. Roger sent an autobiographical manuscript to family and friends detailing his frustrations over not having a girlfriend and his hatred for women.

Roger, who had well documented mental health problems, having seen multiple therapists since he was eight years old, may have been a misogynist.

In 2011, he splashed his latte on two girls waiting at a bus stop for not paying attention to him. At one point he told people at a party he attempted pushing some girls over a ledge after being mocked.

In his manifesto, written on April 30, 2014 some three weeks before his rampage, he described his plan to kill people. He complained he was still a virgin at age 22 and had never even kissed a girl.

To say the three men listed above were mentally ill is painfully obvious, but the common thread in their illness is their problems with women. This thread may be a clue to identifying potential mass killers. This thread certainly underscores the need for a new, massive commitment to mental health care.

The problem in analyzing the causes of school shootings is it often reveals a generous helping of incompetence and ignorance on the part of senior law enforcement, school, and mental health officials. This is the case in the Appalachian School of Law murders and the Virginia Tech rampage.

To quote Douglas Kellner in his book, *Guys and Guns Run Amock*, "Complex events always have a multiplicity of causes and to attempt to produce a single-factor explanation or solution is simplistic and reductive."

So yes, part of the solution begins with enforcing the laws and rules we have in place. There is no excuse for failing to tackle the plethora of causes behind the growing number of school shootings.

All of Us Have Rights

A potentially dangerous student on campus does have rights, but we must be careful not to overstate those rights. Nowhere is a dangerous student given the right to kill innocent people.

The actions so far in dealing with gun violence, especially school shootings, expose hesitancy on the part of people in authority. Public and elected officials appear only willing to take half-measures. Time and time again there is a desire to avoid offending powerful interests. Protecting the careers of prominent politicians, law enforcement officials, and school leaders appears to be the motivation for this inaction. The net result is an unholy trinity of lies, deceit, and cover-ups.

Douglas Kellner's book has another poignant quote from the highly reputable British news magazine, *The Economist*. "*It (The Economist) indicated that while disturbed people exist in every society, the difference, 'as everyone knows but no one in authority was saying this week, is that in America such individuals have easy access to weapons of terrible destructive power. Cho killed his victims with two guns, one of them a Glock 9mm semi-automatic pistol, a rapid-fire weapon is available only to police in virtually every other country, but which can legally be bought over the counter in thousands of gun shops in America. There are estimated to be 240 million guns in America, considerably more than there are adults, and around a third of them are handguns, easy to conceal and use. Had powerful guns not been available to him, the deranged Cho would have killed fewer people, and perhaps none at all.'*"

If there is no silver bullet, then when do we begin a meaningful dialog to find ways to curb gun violence?

"Now Is Not The Time"

Following the shooting at Newtown, Connecticut, then-Speaker of the House John Boehner said, "Now is not the time" to discuss these shootings. I would argue there is no better time to begin a serious dialog than after the hideous massacre of first graders and their teachers.

When we hear the phrase, "now is not the time" we must question "Ok, if not now, when?". Tell us and we will be there. We will come armed with proposals to keep guns out of the hands of those who are a threat to themselves and others: We will come prepared to discuss mental health issues, ways to identify and remove mediocre university and college officials, and any subject to end this violence.

Chapter 6

Shell Games And Lies

One excuse after another is all you get when you ask why can't something be done to stop the gun violence; why can't something be done to prevent our schools from becoming shooting galleries.

The bottom line is, when it comes to guns, the Second Amendment champions want absolutely no restrictions on gun ownership, and laws with little or no accountability. As noted in the previous chapter, the most common excuse heard for inaction is we need to enforce the laws we have. Yes, we do need to enforce existing laws. But the gun advocates stop there; they don't want any laws with a bite in them. They won't agree to enforce the laws holding people accountable.

Some gun advocates are so extreme in their laissez-faire attitudes if you follow their line of reasoning to its ultimate conclusion, they would end up defending Adam Lanza's right to own as many guns as he wanted.

Second Amendment

Second Amendment advocates engage in a variety of word and phrase shell games. The most common game centers on the argument: *guns don't kill, people do*. Of course guns don't kill; they are inanimate objects. Inanimate objects only kill in people's hands. Keeping guns out of the hands of convicted felons, terrorists, people who are a threat to themselves and others, is critical to keeping all of us safe. Yet when you suggest some sort of background check to identify these people, the gun lobbyists cry foul. They claim such a check would violate people's civil rights. I never hear them talk about the civil rights of students and theatergoers who have been killed or wounded.

The Patriotism Game

The Second Amendment advocates call themselves "patriots." They have delegated to themselves the right to determine who is and who is not a patriot based upon an individual's support for unfettered access to all guns.

It is my belief that you cannot consider yourself a patriot when you militate for the unfettered access to all guns, giving a green light to terrorists, criminals, and those who are a danger of harming themselves and others. Perhaps they should step back and examine what happens when anyone can buy guns anywhere at any time. Terrorist groups such as al Qa'ida could direct their operatives in the U.S. to "Go to a gun show in Virginia, and buy as many guns as you want. There will be no background check."

It doesn't sound patriotic to me to take a position defending the right of Adam Lanza, Seung Hui Cho or James Holmes to own guns and massacre innocent students, teachers or theatergoers.

Manipulating Patriots

The Second Amendment advocates appear oblivious to the fact there are other Amendments to the Constitution, and all of them have limitations. There are limits on my freedom of speech. I cannot slander someone or go around using foul or offensive language without paying a price.

Those who play the patriotism game don't stop to consider what weapons were available in the latter half of the 18th century. For the founding fathers, muskets were the state of the art guns. It is impossible to carry out a mass killing with a musket. The founding fathers, in their wildest dreams, could not have imagined today's guns with magazines capable of holding hundreds of rounds of ammunition.

The Second Amendment advocates don't realize they are being manipulated. The word games and lies are being used against them to make the gun manufacturers rich. The NRA and gun manufacturers promote fear. They convince the timid the government is coming to confiscate everyone's guns. This isn't a word game; it is a lie.

Bastrop, Texas

Newspaper stories in the *Boston Globe* and *Chicago Tribune* in the spring and summer of 2015 reported the people of Bastrop, Texas believed the Obama Administration and the U.S. military were coming to take their weapons. I thought it was a joke. Sadly, it was not.

Some politicians in Bastrop, Texas warned their fellow citizens to prepare; the U.S. government was coming to seize their weapons in connection with a large-scale military exercise covering several western states. Let's look at the facts:

- Yes, the U.S. military was preparing to conduct the largest multistate exercises in its history.

- Yes, the exercises were and did take place from July 15 to September 15, 2015.

- No, the government did not confiscate anybody's weapons.

Before the exercise, the press quoted a right-wing politician who stated a U.S. military's exercise was part of an Obama Administration "plan to spy on them, confiscate their guns and ultimately establish martial law."

Just how paranoid can people be? Could there be so many emotionally disturbed people in Bastrop, Texas who would believe these absurdities?

According to the press, Bastrop County Judge Paul Pape tried to reassure the county's approximately 78,000 citizens that the federal government was not coming to take their guns. He tried to reason with them that the exercise was routine. But his efforts were met with placards reading, "No Gestapo in Bastropo."

Really? Has anyone told the people of Bastrop the U.S. government has heavy artillery, drones, and nuclear weapons? The U.S. government is coming after Bastrop, Texas? Bastrop residents are going to take rifles and pistols to a drone and missile fight?

And why would anyone (outside of the town residents), especially the U.S. government, care about Bastrop? The President and Washington politicians have to worry about al Qa'ida, ISIL, the Greek financial crisis, drug trafficking, growing strains with Russia, this country's huge China debt, closing the earnings gap in this country, and a truck load of other major economic and political problems. Does anyone really believe President Obama and Washington politicians are willing to put those problems on the back burner so they can concentrate on Bastrop, Texas? Does anyone outside of Bastrop even know where the town is?

The Bureau of Alcohol, Tobacco, and Firearms (ATF) estimates there are around 350 million guns in the U.S. According to some media outlets, 10 million guns are manufactured in the U.S. each year and another 5 million are imported. There are less than 3,000 ATF agents. If the ATF is going to come knocking on your door, you can expect a visit in 50 or 60 years.

Just how many enemies do these people in Bastrop have? Why do they need to be armed to the teeth?

The people of Bastrop should not be afraid of Washington; they should be afraid of some of their neighbors who appear to be hell-bent on living in an armed world of self-aggrandizing paranoia. Furthermore, some of Bastrop's politicians appear to be 40-watt appliance bulbs—they are the real threat to public safety and citizen's rights, not the politicians in Washington.

Bastrop has become an advertisement for the importance of heavy spending on better education and mental health care.

Corrupting the Constitution

We do not use the First Amendment to ensure the media makes a profit or to keep newspapers, radio and TV stations in business. We should not use the Second Amendment to ensure profits for gun manufacturers. That is exactly what is happening.

If any of the founding fathers came back to life I find it hard to believe they would support allowing those who are a threat to themselves and others to own assault rifles and weapons with high capacity clips. Those weapons were designed for the military and the police. They are designed to kill people, not to be used for home defense.

Selectively Citing the Founding Fathers

I would also remind the Second Amendment advocates the founding fathers wrote more than just the Second Amendment. If you look at the *Declaration of Independence*, written by the founding fathers, it contains the following words:

We hold these truths to be self-evident, that all men are created equal, they are endowed by their Creator with certain unalienable Rights, that among these are Life, Liberty and the pursuit of Happiness.

There are then, many rights guaranteed to U.S. citizens by the founding fathers, including the right to "life, liberty and the pursuit of happiness." I would remind the Second Amendment advocates the *Declaration of Independence* predates the *Constitution*. The right to life was first and foremost on their minds; the right to bear arms came later.

Even in the Amendments to the *Constitution*, the first deals with freedom of speech. It would appear the founding fathers put the right to life and free speech ahead of the right to own guns and the right to bear arms was meant to defend life and personal safety, not to be used by neighborhood vigilantes to take lives.

The Second Amendment advocates never mention the rights of those killed or wounded. It bothers me deeply.

Willful Blindness

Willful blindness is a term used in criminal law referring to someone who intentionally fails to be informed about matters, making the person criminally liable. The phrase describes an "attempt to avoid civil or criminal liability for a wrongful act by intentionally putting oneself in a position to be unaware of facts which create liability." Willful blindness often masquerades as "I don't remember," "I don't recall," or "I forget."

"Willful blindness" is conscious avoidance of the truth. Unfortunately, the conscious avoidance of the truth has been a prime characteristic of authorities in Virginia before, during, and after both school shootings in the *Old Dominion*. In the case of the Appalachian School of Law, school authorities feigned lack of knowledge the killer was violent, despite overwhelming evidence to the contrary.

In the case of Virginia Tech, school officials made similar claims. The loss of memory on the part of police, health care, and school authorities reached near epidemic proportions. Dr. Cathye Betzel, a licensed clinical psychologist, cannot remember her conversation about Cho's disturbing behavior with English Department Chairperson Lucinda Roy. Professor Roy remembers it quite well.

Virginia Tech Police Chief Wendell Flinchum remained silent for months about the timing of when Virginia Tech had a person of interest following the double homicide in West Ambler Johnston Hall shortly after 7:00 a.m. The discrepancy (the school said it identified a person of interest before 7:30 a.m. when in fact it was approximately an hour later), gave the school a fig leaf excuse for not locking down and warning.

Virginia Tech's Police Chief Flinchum's lie of omission made it all the way into the first version of the Governor's Review Panel Report. Lying by omission, also known as exclusionary detailing, is defined as lying by either omitting certain facts or by failing to correct a misconception.

If you read the transcript of the trial against Virginia Tech in the lawsuit of the Pryde and Peterson families who lost their daughters on April 16, 2007, the school and police officials repeatedly cannot remember, or do not recall. It is as if collective dementia struck Blacksburg and the Virginia Tech campus with a vengeance.

Honing the Lies

Since Angie's death fourteen years ago, a small fortune has been spent on electronic security equipment to improve school safety, giving the public a false sense of security.

In most of the shootings I have examined the human factor is the critical flaw, not the policies or the warning systems. Yes, the latter two needed improvement and more needs to be done. But it was a breakdown in the decision making process on the part of one or more human beings that sealed the fate of most of the victims.

At the Appalachian School of Law, its President brushed aside calls for campus security. At Virginia Tech, the school's President and Police Chief not only broke the school's security policies, but they violated the basic tenants of crime scene investigation and procedures and did not warn. Everywhere I look at a school shooting it always comes back to human flaw: incompetence coupled with bad judgment.

The most notable progress I can see since Angela Dales was murdered thirteen years ago is the ability and willingness of people to obfuscate, manipulate words, and cover-up. The shell games and lies discussed in this chapter set the stage for the most disappointing of all the revelations in the last thirteen plus years, the corruption in our legal and judicial systems. I discuss these topics in the next chapter.

The Oxymoron

Perhaps the most insidious deception played on the public is by state and federal legislatures. And, the Virginia House of Delegates excels at pulling the wool over the eyes of the public when it comes to domestic abuse and gun violence.

This is what I am talking about: On July 16, 2016 a new provision of the law prohibits a person who is subject to a family abuse protection order (the respondent) from possessing a firearm. Sounds good, but is it?

Let's take a close look.

After the respondent is served with the protective order, the law states he or she has 24 hours to lawfully possess the weapon solely for the purpose of transferring or selling the firearm to a person who may legally own it. The law does not give the police the power to confirm the person being restrained complies with the order. If the respondent says he turned the gun in, sold it, or gave it to someone who can possess the gun, law enforcement has to believe him. There is no mechanism for ensuring the person being restrained has truly complied.

Furthermore, if an individual is so violent that the courts have to step in, what makes the legislature think the respondent will suddenly cool off and meekly comply?

Furthermore, the law only applies to subjects of family abuse protective orders pursuant to Virginia Code Section 16.1-279.1 and does not apply to individuals subject to an emergency, temporary or other protective order.

The law is, at best, window dressing and is next to worthless.

The America
We All Want

Part 3

Investigations without
integrity are worthless

Chapter 7

More Corrupt Than I Thought

If it is not independent, it is not worthy of trust. Investigations have to have integrity and they have to have fairness. If they don't have that, they are not dependable for anyone.

John Dowd
Former MLB Special Counsel

Since Angela Dales' murder at the Appalachian School of Law on January 16, 2002, we, as a nation, appeared to have lowered our standards. It is relatively easy for people with low intellect, little character, and a healthy dose of incompetence to buy the people we have put our trust in—our politicians, lawyers, and judges. When I did my research for this chapter the magnitude of the dishonesty and corruption was shocking. The situation is stunningly distressing.

Victimizing the Victims

Just when you think the gun manufacturers and National Rifle Association (NRA) have sunk about as low as they can go, they come up with something even more outrageous: Make dead victims' families pay court costs of any legal action.

The gun makers and NRA have undercut public safety by their long history of engaging in nefarious lobbying activity. Now they have persuaded politicians to adopt laws making the victims of gun violence pay the legal fees for challenging what appears to be their self-proclaimed, sacrosanct position.

In September 2014, the *Brady Center* announced a lawsuit on behalf of Sandy and Lonnie Phillips, accusing Web site companies of negligence for selling weapons to the Aurora, Colorado theater shooter, James Holmes. The Phillips daughter, Jessica Ghawi, was killed in the shooting. The lawsuit charged the companies with negligence for selling weapons (including ammunition, body armor, tear gas and other equipment used in this assault) to someone as obviously unstable as Holmes. Holmes ended up killing 12 and wounding 70 others on July 20, 2012 at a movie theater in Aurora, Colorado.

Senior U.S. District Judge Richard P. Matsch of the District of Colorado dismissed the Phillips' suit against four Web sites because Colorado and federal laws shield firearms and ammunition sellers from liability based on a customer's wrongful acts. Phillips et al. v. Lucky Gunner LLC et al., No. 14–cv–02822, 2015 WL 1499382 (D. Colo. Mar. 27, 2015).

Both federal and Colorado laws protect gun makers and sellers from being held responsible for selling arms to people who are a danger to themselves and others. Colorado, however, has taken this a step further, requiring plaintiffs to pay the court costs of the gun makers and sellers.

Lucky Gunner and Sportsman Guide (two of the companies selling to Holmes) have already filed motions for $220,000 in legal costs. According to press reports, another arms dealer, BTP Arms, wants $33,000. BTP Arms request will probably fail because the law does not cover the two tear gas grenades Holmes bought from BTP Arms, nor does the law cover the four pieces of body armor he bought from bulletproofbodyarmorhq.com.

The Phillips' lawsuit underscores this reality: the average citizen is nearly helpless in the face of the wealth and power of the NRA, gun manufacturers, and gun sellers. The Phillips' lawsuit is a shocking example of the disadvantaged position of the average citizen. There is virtually no recourse against the power elite—weapons manufacturers and the gun lobby.

Public Corruption Par Excellence

I have always taught my students that our judges and justices, despite their personal leanings (conservative or liberal) would, in the end, let the facts and evidence of the case guide their decisions. I have been terribly wrong.

As some of you might know, the Pryde and Peterson families, parents of the students killed at Virginia Tech, refused to settle with the state. They filed a lawsuit, not to get money, but to get people under oath and to bring the facts out into the open.

The trial was a devastating indictment of Virginia Tech. On March 14, 2012, a jury awarded the two families $4 million each. But Virginia has sovereign immunity and the judge had to reduce the award to $100,000 each.

The money was not the issue; it was never the issue. The two families wanted to get the truth out and the school's incompetence exposed.

Then-Virginia Attorney General Ken Cuccinelli appealed the decision to the Virginia Supreme Court, one of the most conservative state supreme courts in the nation. This Virginia court believes there are few situations where a person or organization can be held responsible for someone else's actions.

I felt the case against the school was so overpowering that even the Virginia Supreme Court could do nothing else but uphold the jury verdict. Indeed, it is rare for a Supreme Court to overturn a jury verdict. But in what appears to a politically motivated action, the Virginia Supreme Court did, and broke the law, overturned the ruling in an error-ridden decision.

It is against the law for a Supreme Court justice to introduce false evidence into a case or the review of a decision. But that is exactly what Justice Cleo E. Powell's decision did. On October 13, 2013, Justice Powell and all the Court Justices, in a unanimous decision, signed off on a decision overturning the jury verdict.

Page two of the reversal contains a critical factual error. Justice Powell wrote on the morning of April 16, 2007, "Although officers from the Virginia Tech Police Department were the first on the scene, the Blacksburg Police Department led the investigation." is not true.

The Virginia Tech Police Department under Chief Wendell Flinchum was in charge. There is a legal agreement between Blacksburg and the school stating, the police department (Virginia Tech) requesting assistance will retain control of the investigation.

I have a letter from Blacksburg Police Chief Kim Crannis stating the investigation was conducted in accordance with the agreement. I have that agreement. I also have read the five volumes of the trial and both Chief Crannis and Chief Flinchum testified under oath that Chief Flinchum was in charge.

I believe Justice Powell has broken the law, obstructed justice, and violated two Canons of the *Canons of Judicial Conduct for the State of Virginia*. They are Canons 1 and 2.

CANON 1.

A JUDGE SHALL UPHOLD THE INTEGRITY AND INDEPENDENCE OF THE JUDICIARY.

A.

An independent and honorable judiciary is indispensable to justice in our society. A judge should participate in establishing, maintaining and enforcing high standards of conduct, and shall personally observe those standards so that the integrity and independence of the judiciary will be preserved. The provisions of these Canons are to be construed and applied to further that objective.

Although judges should be independent, they must comply with the law, including the provisions of these Canons. Public confidence in the impartiality of the judiciary is maintained by the adherence of each judge to this responsibility. Conversely, violation of this Canon diminishes public confidence in the judiciary and thereby does injury to the system of government under law.

I am not accusing Justice Powell of lying, but by writing a decision containing a factual error of this magnitude (involving the worst school shooting in this nation's history), she has done irreparable harm to "an independent and honorable judiciary [which] is indispensable to justice in our society." She has violated Canon 1. If Justice Powell were a student in one of my classes, I would flunk her.

CANON 2.

A JUDGE SHALL AVOID IMPROPRIETY AND THE APPEARANCE OF IMPROPRIETY IN ALL OF THE JUDGE'S ACTIVITIES.

A.

A judge shall respect and comply with the law and shall act at all times in a manner that promotes public confidence in the integrity and impartiality of the judiciary.

It is against the law to introduce false or wrong facts into court proceedings. By wittingly or unwittingly allowing a factual error into her decision, Justice Powell has, at minimum, been complicit in the violation of the laws of the State of Virginia. This is tantamount to the impropriety of the first order and does not promote "public confidence in the integrity and impartiality of the judiciary." Furthermore, Justice Powell's decision casts serious doubts on the integrity, thoroughness, and objectivity of the Supreme Court of Virginia. The decision should be withdrawn and the verdict of the Circuit Court of Montgomery County, Virginia should be reinstated.

Why Important

This error is important because, as stated above, it is against the law to introduce false evidence into any court proceeding. It is important because the Virginia Supreme Court has re-written history. The Blacksburg police chief did not have the authority to warn and lockdown the campus. Powell's decision alters the historical record, obscuring the fact Virginia Tech Police Chief Flinchum failed in his duties to the school, faculty, staff, and students.

I have read the five-volume transcript of the Pryde and Peterson trial proceedings and nowhere is there reference to Chief Crannis being in charge of the investigation.

Below are two examples of the testimony, taken directly from the trial transcripts, stating Virginia Tech Police Chief Wendell Flinchum was in charge of the investigation:

Virginia Tech Police Chief Wendell Flinchum's testimony he was in charge of the investigation:

Q: I want to be clear about this, this was a Virginia Tech police investigation. Is that correct?

A: It was, yes.

Q: And you were in charge and you were responsible.

A: I was responsible, yes. ...

Blacksburg Police Chief Kimberly Crannis's testimony that Flinchum was in charge of the investigation:

Q: This was a Virginia Tech investigation, right?

A: Yes, it was.

Q: And Chief Flinchum was in charge?

A: Yes, he was.

Q: But you were providing support as you just indicated?

A: Yes, sir.

Q: The conclusion that you tentatively reached with respect to a domestic homicide that you just testified to, was that a topic of conversation between you and Chief Flinchum?

A: Yes, it was. ...

Everything Was In Place To Warn

The identity of who was in charge is critical to understanding what happened on April 16, 2007. The school had all the means necessary to warn and lockdown the campus. Over two and one half hours elapsed between the double homicide and the mass murder in Norris Hall. There was plenty of time to warn and to lockdown. So, the question persists, why did Justice Powell allow erroneous evidence into her ruling? The basic question remains unanswered, why didn't the university issue a warning?

Eight months before the Tech rampage, the Virginia Tech administration had set a standard for warning the university community. In the fall of 2006, a prisoner in the Blacksburg jail, William Morva, escaped and killed two people. There was no indication Morva was on or near the campus, yet Virginia Tech warned and locked the campus down.

On April 16, 2007, there was a double murder in the middle of the campus. Thirteen bloody foot prints led from the crime scene to an exit stairwell; there were spent bullet shells on the floor but no weapon. The school issued no warning even though it was obvious the killer was on the loose. Had a lockdown of the campus been implemented, lives would have been saved. The administrative failure allowed two students to go to their French class where they were among the first of the 30 students and teachers killed in Norris Hall.

The Virginia Supreme Court declined to hold anyone accountable for incompetence in the Virginia Tech massacre. The Court is entitled to its opinions, but not its own facts.

So Much For The ACLU

On November 3, 2014, I sent a letter to Claire Guthrie Gastanaga, Executive Director of the ACLU in Richmond, Virginia, asking if her organization would help me with my complaint against Virginia Supreme Court Justice Cleo E. Powell.

I met Ms. Gastanaga in White Stone, Virginia where I asked her to look at my argument. Her body language clearly indicated she did not welcome my request, but because I asked in the presence of others, she agreed to look at it. She also said she is a personal friend of Justice Powell. I naively hoped she would see the merits in my case, and would refer the complaint to someone else in the ACLU.

It is now over two years since I wrote Ms. Gastanaga. She has not responded and apparently does not intend to acknowledge my letter. In this case it is especially disappointing because of the ACLU's high professional standards.

> **"ACLU MISSION STATEMENT**. Since its founding in 1920, the **American Civil Liberties Union (ACLU)** has been the guardian of liberty, working in the nation's courts, legislatures and communities to defend and preserve individual working rights and liberties guaranteed by the Constitution and the laws of the United States."

Judicial Inquiry And Review Commission

On January 17, 2015, I filed a complaint against Justice Powell and the Virginia Supreme Court with the *Judicial Inquiry and Review Commission*. I included my evidence to support my contention the law had been broken and Justice Powell had probably broken the two Canons of Judicial Conduct cited above.

Here is the response I got:

> *Mr. David Cariens*
> *Kilmarnock, Va. 22482*

> *Dear Mr. Cariens:*

> *This is in response to your complaint to the judicial inquiry and review commission, dated January 17, 2015, alleging a justice issued an erroneous opinion in an appeal. The commission has no authority to review a judge's rulings and decisions.*

> *Sincerely,*

> *S/Robert Q. Harris*
> *Assistant Counsel*

The problem with Mr. Harris' response is the *Judicial Inquiry and Review Commission* does have the right to investigate whether or not someone, in this case a Justice of the Supreme Court, has broken the law.

Virginia Attorney General—No Answer

Surely someone must be interested in the Virginia Supreme Court re-writing history and in so doing breaking the law. Unfortunately, I would be proven wrong again.

On January 19, 2015 I wrote the Virginia Attorney General laying out my evidence and asking him to investigate whether or not Justice Powell and the Virginia Supreme Court had broken the law.

The following are excerpts from my letter to Virginia Attorney General Herring:

> *I have filed a complaint with the judicial inquiry and review commission against Virginia Supreme Court Justice Cleo E. Powell. The complaint centers on a major factual error in her October 31, 2013 decision to throw out the jury verdict holding Virginia Tech liable in the Pryde and Peterson lawsuit against the school. (my complaint and the evidence are attached).*

> *Justice Powell wrote that the Blacksburg police were in charge of the investigation of the killings on April 16, 2007, but in fact it was the Virginia Tech Police Department. I have been involved in and teach intelligence and crime analysis for nearly 50 years. … this is a stunning factual error … if one of my students made this mistake I would flunk him or her.*

> *Both Blacksburg Police Chief Kim Crannis and Virginia Tech Police Chief Wendell Flinchum testified under oath that it was the Virginia Tech Police who were in charge. (the testimony is included in the complaint.)*

> *The question arises how could such an error of this magnitude make it into the Supreme Court's decision when the evidence before the court states the opposite? Indeed, there are at least five references in the testimony that the Virginia Tech Police Department was in charge.*

> *It is against the law to introduce false evidence or facts in a court of law. It must certainly be against the law to feed false facts to a Supreme Court Justice; facts that are contained in a ruling involving the worst school shooting in this nation's history. The error is so great that it casts doubt on the court's integrity, objectivity, and truthfulness.*

I am not accusing Justice Powell and the court of being untruthful, but I am arguing that for this ruling to stand uncorrected is tantamount to condoning factual errors at the highest level of the state's judiciary.

Because of the factual error in the Pryde and Peterson decision, there is a very real possibility that the two families' civil rights were violated. There is also the possibility of some form of public corruption in the form of undue influence on the court.

I am asking that the Attorney General's Office investigate whether or not there is a civil rights violation and how a factual error on that scale could make it into a major Virginia Supreme Court decision.

It is now more than sixteen months later, and I have received no response.

The FBI

Undaunted, but somewhat discouraged, I asked some colleagues at the FBI if there was any merit to my argument and evidence.

The answer was "yes." They described the introduction of factual evidence into a Supreme Court decision as grounds for charges of public corruption and encouraged me to take my case to the FBI Richmond office. I then talked with an FBI special agent who investigates public corruption in a major U.S. city. He said, "Absolutely, this needs to be investigated."

In April 2015, I met with an FBI Special Agent in Richmond for over an hour and laid out my case. He explained he did not handle public corruption, but would hand my complaint over to those who do.

In February 2016, I received a call from the FBI. They have accepted the complaint and an investigation has been opened. The fact the complaint has been accepted means the lawyers at the Bureau's office in Richmond believe it has merit.

Furthermore, a source at the FBI in Quantico told me he believes that because a Virginia Supreme Court Justice is the target, the complaint was probably run by the Department of Justice in Washington, D.C. before it was accepted.

I was also told to be patient; it may take nine months or more for the bureau to do it's investigation as to whether or not to indite the Justice.

Chapter 8

How Much Is Your Child Worth?

In Virginia, apparently not much.

The cards are stacked against parents if their child is wounded or killed on a campus or school grounds in Virginia. In fact, if your child is the victim of a crime, any crime, it is hard to get justice in the Virginia legal system.

First, you begin with the points I discussed in the preceding chapter; most Virginia judges and justices take the position no one can be held accountable for anyone else's actions. And the laws are written to reflect bias. Second, politicians on both sides of the aisle in Richmond appear unwilling to tackle the multiple problems. This has led to campus gun violence—the nearly unrestricted access to guns, the sharp decline in the availability and quality of mental health care, and the willingness of people to play fast and free with the truth.

Following Angie Dales murder fourteen years ago, we tried, and eventually got, compensation for our then seven-year-old granddaughter. Virginia has sovereign immunity, meaning you cannot sue the state for more than $100,000. The Appalachian School of Law, however, was not a state school; it was not protected by sovereign immunity.

An out-of-court settlement was reached between Angie's parents and the law school. The school agreed to pay $1 million to the plaintiffs. Angie's mother and father had joined forces with the three wounded students, so the money was split four ways. Our then seven-year-old granddaughter got the lion's share, over $300,000, thus ensuring her education. We were fortunate.

Virginia Tech

Five years after Angie's murder, the nation's worst mass shooting occurred at Virginia Tech, less than 200 miles from the law school. Despite the expressions of sympathy and crocodile tears, Virginia Tech officials as well as politicians of all stripes came together in a cauldron of deceit, dishonesty, and political larceny.

Virginia Tech is a state school and protected by sovereign immunity. The largest judgment anyone can win against the state, with few exceptions, is $100,000. In reality, the state is willing to spend millions of dollars to protect incompetent and inept university administrators, but not one cent more than $100,000 to the dead students' parents or the spouses of dead professors or instructors.

Let's look at how Virginia Tech spent its money in order to spin the tragedy to its benefit and conceal the incompetence of the school's leadership:

Virginia Tech paid $150,000 to the public relations firm, *Firestorm,* for 10 days work to help the school begin to spin the tragedy to its benefit.

Virginia Tech paid $663,000 to an even bigger public relations firm when it became clear the negative publicity about the school was too big for *Firestorm* to handle. The firm was *Bursen-Marsteller,* the same public relations firm who was the spin-doctor for *Dow-Corning's* campaign to limit damages arising from their silicone breast implants. The same *Bursen-Marsteller* who had been hired by big tobacco companies to develop a campaign to defuse the bad publicity associated with smoking.

Virginia (unlike Colorado in the case of Columbine and Connecticut in the case of Sandy Hook) hired a private company to write the report analyzing the Virginia Tech shooting and determining if the school was culpable. The firm was *TriData,* an Arlington, Virginia based company doing business with the state. The state paid *TriData* over $600,000 to produce a badly flawed report. The state then paid *TriData* another $75,000 to issue two corrected, subsequent versions. The final version still contains errors.

As noted above, the families of the dead students and faculty each got $100,000. You should also know the 30 families of the deceased agreed to settle with the state only after lawyers from the state's Attorney General's office made it clear they would hold up paying the medical bills for the wounded until a settlement was reached.

The lawyers representing the families received over $1 million.

Two Virginia Tech families who lost daughters on April 16, 2007 and would not settle with the state, sued. They won a jury verdict, but the Virginia Supreme Court, as cited earlier in this book, overturned the decision. The Pryde and Peterson families got $0.

The Hokie Spirit Memorial Fund

Since the shooting at the Appalachian School of Law on January 16, 2002, I have learned there is no end to the extent of some people's greed. The *Hokie Spirit Memorial Fund*, is an especially unsavory look into the unscurpulous mindset of the school and state leadership.

Soon after the shooting, Virginia Tech established the *Hokie Spirit Memorial Fund*. Billed as a tribute to the dead and wounded, people could show their support to the school and the victims by making contributions to the fund.

Across the country people opened their hearts and their pocket books. The money rolled in—millions of dollars. Virginia Tech must have thought it had found the pot of gold at the end of the rainbow.

The school said $8.5 million represented the bulk of the funds received; in fact the figure was around $160 million. (For a breakdown of the facts and figures associated with the *Hokie Spirit Memorial Fund*, see chapter 10 of *Virginia Tech: Make Sure It Doesn't Get Out.*)

Larceny?

There were reports stating if contributors did not write *Hokie Spirit Memorial Fund* on the check's memo line, the money was deposited in the school's general fund. There were also reports, again never denied by the school, Virginia Tech informally told major contributors not to contribute until after the *Hokie Spirit Memorial Fund* closed because the money would then go directly to the school. The families would not see a penny of it; nor would the scholarships memorializing those killed. Even with regard to the $8.5 million in the fund, the families had next to no say in how the money was distributed or how it was spent.

With the handling of the *Hokie Spirit Memorial Fund,* the Virginia Tech school administrator's repugnant behavior—a willingness to line the school's pockets on the murder of 32 people.

Mental Health Care

Everyone agrees the quality of available mental health care is part of the answer to stemming the tide of school shootings. Yet, in the fourteen years since the shooting at the Appalachian School of Law the quality of mental health care in Virginia has declined; thanks in a large part to the privatization of mental health care facilities.

What better example does anyone need than the sloppy and unprofessional care given Seung Hui Cho in the years and months before he went on his rampage?

The Deeds Tragedy

The tragedy that struck the Creigh Deeds family on November 19, 2014 is, in part, the result of a failed Virginia policy toward mental health. Both sides of the political aisle in Richmond are to blame.

According to press reports, Austin "Gus" Deeds had a mental-health evaluation on Monday November 18, 2013 and an Emergency Custody Order, ECO, had been placed on Gus Deeds to see if he should be placed in custody for a longer period. Mental health officials said they could not find a bed to hold young Deeds for further evaluation and treatment. It was not true. Subsequently, it was found out beds were available. The next morning young Deeds apparently had a psychotic episode and stabbed his father multiple times in the face and upper torso before killing himself.

Austin "Gus" Deeds died, in part, because of the poorly run private mental care system in Virginia; a system that cannot even keep track of vacant beds. Young Austin Deeds was a victim of political machinations in Richmond. Politicians who have backed cuts in mental health treatment and the privatization of the state's mental health care share part of the blame for the calamity striking the Deeds family.

McDonnell's Promises

Following the Virginia Tech massacre, state officials promised more money and more emphasis on mental health. They kept their promise—for one year. Virginia now spends less on mental health than it did on April 16, 2007. In fact, former Governor Bob McDonnell's policy of privatizing the state's mental health care was an attack on the most vulnerable segment of society, the portion of the population least able to defend itself—the mentally ill.

Privatization is not advocated in order to improve health care. It is pursued to curry favor with those who want to minimize government no matter what the cost—in this case, a human life.

Politicizing Mental Health Care

Unfortunately, the need for more and better mental health care is being politicized.

The National Review could not resist distorting the facts and demonizing those with whom they disagree. In a recent editorial the magazine wrote, "The common thread in these tragedies is not the killer's choice of weapons, but his unhinged state of mind." It would sound as if the influential conservative magazine is throwing its editorial weight behind expanding and improving mental health care.

Unfortunately it is not the case.

The magazine could not resist lambasting liberals. The next sentence reads, "Liberals pushed the 'de-institutionalization' movement of the 1960s made it almost impossible to keep mentally ill people safely locked up." The *National Review* is distorting the facts. Large state and federal mental health facilities existed well into the 1980s.

Both liberals and conservatives played roles in closing mental health facilities. This policy has led to the plummeting of the quality of mental health care.

New Jersey and Virginia, the two states I am familiar with, have closed mental health hospitals with disastrous results. Both states have privatized mental health care and the result has been a marked decline in the quality and amount of mental health treatment.

What a shame a major national magazine couldn't resist trying to score points on the bodies of students, staff, and faculty.

In the final analysis, we don't need to waste time and energy arguing whose fault it is. Our mental health care system is underfunded and woefully inadequate. We need to stop blaming each other for past mistakes and turn our attention to stopping the gun violence epidemic.

We need liberals and conservatives to stop pointing fingers at each other and come together in the common cause of ending school shootings.

Fourteen Years Later

So, fourteen years after the murder of Angela Dales, the harsh reality is abundantly clear: the average family has little recourse in Virginia if their child is killed on a school campus. I have learned politicians in Richmond lack the courage to find the root of the problem and tell the truth about gun violence in Virginia in general, and school shootings specifically.

From mental health care to campus security, Virginia's elected officials appear to be happy playing Russian roulette with the lives of young people, students, teachers, and professors. Children apparently are worth next to nothing in the eyes of the political leaders in Richmond, even if gross incompetence led to their deaths.

No amount of money can ever replace a child or loved one. Given a choice, you could not give a parent any amount of money for the life of a child. But in Virginia, the state places an insulting price tag on the life of a child--$100,000. Compare this figure to the salaries of school presidents posted on *VirginiaWatchdog.org*:

Virginia Commonwealth University President Michael Rao received a $275,000 signing bonus when he inked his employment contract in October 2012, with $200,000 a year in deferred compensation. This is in addition to a base salary just shy of half a million dollars.

Whenever Christopher Newport University President Paul Tribble leaves his presidential post, he'll continue making whatever his final base salary is — more than $360,000 — to teach just three courses over the entire academic year as a tenured professor at the Newport News institution.

According to the *Chronicle of Higher Education*'s national ranking of executive leadership by compensation, recently retired Virginia Tech President Charles Steger made $836,886 during fiscal year 2013. His salary alone placed him as the 12th highest-paid public college president in the U.S. out of 256 institutions.

Charles Steger was the president of Virginia Tech on April 16, 2007. He and then-Police Chief Wendell Flinchum, failed to warn or lockdown the campus following a double homicide at West Ambler Johnston Hall. As a result the killer, Seung Hui Cho, methodically proceeded with his plans and killed 30 students and faculty in Norris Hall two and a half hours later.

- Charles Steger made $836,886 his last year as Virginia Tech president.

- 28 families got $100,000 for their dead children and spouses.

- The Pryde and Peterson families, whose daughters were killed in Norris Hall, got nothing.

Chapter 9

No Value For Life

Since the shooting at the Appalachian School of Law in January 2002, one of the most sobering facts I have come to terms with is the extent mendacity permeates the leadership cadre of our society.

When I was writing the book on the Virginia Tech rampage, I finally stopped my research because every time I picked up a rock, something else crawled out from under. I found few leaders of principle and few working for the common good.

Not On My Watch

Almost everywhere I have looked I found people who were unwilling to take a stand on an issue if they perceive it would damage their careers or the institutions they work for.

University and college officials are not alone in hiding from or concealing the truth; it seems to be everywhere. I was aware of this deploring phenomenon when I worked for the government. More than once, I encountered senior officers who would say, "We don't want to tell the President this," or "The President doesn't want to hear that." They would say this even though the point being made was factually accurate.

In my career as an intelligence analyst, for example, I was told by a senior official to lie about the conclusions of a major study. I was told to say country "x" was in danger of civil war and blood shed. My paper said the opposite.

When I refused, the very annoyed senior official said, "Let me put it this way, Dave, if you say country 'x' is in danger of civil war and blood shed, and it doesn't happen, no one will remember it. This is good for your career. If you say there is little or no threat of civil war in country 'x' and there is war and bloodshed, that is bad for your career and it is bad for my career."

I refused, and eventually won; the paper was published exactly as I wrote it. I paid a price however. I had stood up to and embarrassed a senior manager. I was not promoted for three years.[1*]

It is easy to look the other way; it is hard to take a principled stand. And, remember, no good deed goes unpunished.

The pervasive attitude on the part of school leaders, politicians and many people in positions of authority seem to be "not on my watch; don't let anything happen on my watch to derail my career." Better to look the other way; there is a good chance it will go away.

The extent to which supervisors will ignore problems was also driven home to me when I was a supervisor.

One of my subordinates told me a female colleague was being sexual harassed. When I asked the woman if it was true she being sexually harassed, she said, "yes."

I reported to my supervisor who said he would handle it. After six weeks of silence, and the harassment continuing, I took the problem to the office director, who became furious with me. The office director berated me saying that because of my actions "he would have to do something about it."

In other words, management was telling me I should have kept quiet in hopes the whole problem would go away.

---

1   For a more thorough examination of corruption of Intelligence, *Intelligence and Crime Analysis: Critical Thinking Through Writing*, Chapter 4, *Mistakes, Problems and Pressure*, pages 41-50, High Tide Publications, Deltaville, Virginia, 2015.

Distorting Military Success

Duplicity is everywhere.

As I write, the Pentagon's Inspector General is investigating allegations U.S. military officers are corrupting intelligence assessments to make the campaign against DAISH (ISIL) look more successful. Members of the press, including the *New York Times*, have reported the investigation.

According to the media, the investigation began after a Defense Intelligence Agency analyst provided the Pentagon with evidence showing the U.S. Central Command (CENTCOM) has inflated the success of our policy against DAISH. The false reports were given to U.S. policymakers at all levels, including President Barack Obama.

Government officials familiar with the inquiry told the *New York Times* CENTCOM commanders improperly rewrote the conclusions of some reports to provide a more optimistic account of progress in the fight.

A directive by the Office of the Director of National Intelligence, overseeing all 17 U.S. intelligence agencies bars "distortion" of analytical assessments by particular agendas or policies.

Military Distortions—Nothing New

The current investigation of military intelligence is not the first time our armed forces have distorted intelligence. In 1967, an intense intra-Intelligence Community battle was waged mainly between the CIA and military intelligence in Saigon over the strength of the Viet Cong.

This battle centered on the strength of the Viet Cong prior to the Tet offensive. The CIA had intelligence warning the Viet Cong forces in South Vietnam numbered over 500,000. General Westmoreland's intelligence unit in Saigon, U.S. Military Assistance Command, Vietnam (MACV), insisted the figure was no higher than 300,000.

The dispute culminated in the production of a National Intelligence Estimate in the fall of 1967 that used the MACV figures. The CIA, despite strong opposition from its Vietnam specialists, caved in and went along with the lower figure.

The nagging questions are, would U.S. forces fighting in South Vietnam been better prepared to counter the Tet offensive had they known the enemy's true strength? Would U.S. lives have been saved?

For a thorough examination and analysis of U.S. involvement in Vietnam, see George Allen's *None So Blind*.

Cheaper to Hire A New Professor

Professor Helen de Haven, at Atlanta's John Marshall Law School, has identified a number of problems with school responses to faculty complaints about threatening students. Professor de Haven has done some excellent research and analysis on school shootings. Her articles have appeared in *The Journal of College and University Law*, a peer reviewed journal published by the Notre Dame University Law School.

One of her articles recounts a depressing story by Professor Carol Parker at the University of Tennessee and her colleagues:

A law professor was being stalked and threatened with death by a student who was failing his class. He and his colleague went to the administration. Sadly, he later reported, they simply stuck their heads in the sand and said nothing was happening. For the administration, this do-nothing strategy was a win-win situation. If they took action, they might get sued. However, in the small chance that the student actually carried out his threat and killed the professor, we figured that they would hire a cheaper faculty member. (Smith, Thomas & Parker: Violence on campus practical recommendations for legal education)

Carol Parker's article is accessible free on the social science research network (ssrn).

Penn State

The preceding anecdote strikes at the heart of what appears to be under-the-table actions by a school administration whose main goal appears to be the protection of the school and its reputation—at all costs. Look at Penn State. There were no deaths at State College, but young boys' lives have been scarred forever; they have been psychologically and physically damaged. And how did Penn State's leadership respond? The school thought of the institution first and put protecting the university's reputation ahead of the safety of children. The following is a direct quote from the findings of the Louis Freeh report investigating Penn State sexual abuse scandal:

> *Our most saddening and sobering finding is the total disregard for the safety and welfare of Sandusky's child victims by the most senior leaders at Penn State. The most powerful men at Penn State failed to take any steps for 14 years to protect the children who Sandusky victimized. Messrs. Spanier, Schultz, Paterno and Curley never demonstrated, through actions or words, any concern for the safety and well being of Sandusky's victims until after Sandusky's arrest.*

It appears Penn State responded with a wink and a nod, an incomprehensible willingness to turn a blind eye to child abuse. Both schools—Penn State and Virginia Tech—put the reputations of their respective institutions ahead of taking action. Neither school took the correct course of action when confronted with crimes—Virginia Tech at the double homicide in West Ambler Johnston Hall, nor Penn State when confronted with eyewitness accounts of child abuse.

"Protect the school and its reputation" appears to have been the mantra of these administrations bent on shielding their inactions from review and recriminations.

Look at the Appalachian School of Law, Virginia Tech, and now Penn State. In all three cases, the inaction of school officials struck at the heart of common sense and human decency. In all three instances, at all three schools, the words "mediocre" and "incompetent" leadership describe the actions of the schools' administrations.

Eastern Michigan University

Let's examine yet another example of where a school's wanton disregard for the safety of students is readily apparent. The case against Eastern Michigan University is the highest fine imposed on a school. The school was fined $357,500 for failing to warn the campus of a 2006 student's assault and death.

Eastern Michigan University student Laura Dickinson was murdered by a fellow student on December 13, 2006. Dickinson was found in her room four days after her murder. She was naked, a pillow over her head, and there were traces of semen on one leg. The police later said there was "no reason to suspect foul play." The school therefore did not issue a warning. Ten weeks later, however, student Orange Taylor III was arrested and charged with Dickinson's murder. Taylor's arrest occurred on the first day so students could not withdraw from classes and housing and receive a full refund.

After a thorough investigation, the school was found in violation of *The Clery Act* [2] for not notifying students of the danger. School

2   The Clery Act is named for Jeanne Clery, a 19-year-old Lehigh University student who was raped and murdered in her campus residence hall in 1986. Clery's parents found out students had not been warned of the 38 violent crimes on campus in the three years prior to their daughter's murder. They helped persuade Congress to pass a law making it mandatory to warn students of violent crimes on campus.

President John A. Fallon was fired; no reason was given for his termination, but the press reported it was for his apparent role in the cover up. The Director of Public Safety and Chief of Police were both relieved of their jobs.

On December 13, 2007, the school settled with Laura Dickinson's family for $2.5 million. The school did not admit any guilt. Orange Taylor III was convicted of first-degree murder and sexual assault. He was sentenced to life in prison on May 8, 2008.

There are parallels between the Appalachian School of Law, Eastern Michigan and Virginia Tech. The parallels include the failure of school and police officials to warn a campus when confronted with a student homicide. Yes, the lengths of the delays were completely different, but in both cases of Virginia Tech and Eastern Michigan, the schools trivialized a homicide in order to delay a campus-wide notification. Whether you wait over two hours or over two months to warn is irrelevant—it is inexcusable.

The Clery Act calls for a warning to be given to the campus population when a murder occurs on campus. It does not distinguish between murders by deranged gunmen, murders by rapists and murders caused by a supposed domestic dispute. If someone is found murdered on campus, an immediate warning is called for—lives are at stake.

Chapter 10

What Will It Take?

Following the alarming instances of school shootings in October 2015, the magazine, The Week, devoted the cover of a recent edition to the problem with a blazing headline, The endless vigil: Are we powerless to stop mass killings?

The magazine quoted Nicholas Kristof of the *New York Times*. "No single new law is going to solve the problem of gun violence, but we dramatically cut the rate of auto fatalities through the passage of multiple regulations—requiring driver's licenses, seat belts, air bags, safety glass, etc. If we take the same incremental approach to guns—universal background checks, safe-storage laws, and careful licensing of gun owners—we might save thousands of lives a year. Locking up all angry loners in advance is not an option."

The magazine then added, "We're *all* crazy if we can't take modest steps to reduce the carnage that leaves America resembling a battlefield."

Kristof is correct. We need to begin taking modest steps on a wide variety of fronts in an effort to curb the slaughter; we are all crazy if we don't.

An Uphill Battle

In the absence of politicians and school leaders with backbones, it will be difficult to get legislators to adopt even the most elementary measures to keep guns out of the hands of those who are a threat to themselves or others, terrorists, convicted felons, and spouse abusers.

To quote Douglas Kellner in his book, *Guys and Guns Amock: Domestic*

Terrorism and School Shootings from the Oklahoma City Bombing to the Virginia Tech Massacre: "Given the power of the gun lobby and the cowardice of politicians, obviously only a minimal amount of gun control is foreseeable. Certainly, the attempts at reform after Columbine were advanced during the Clinton-Gore years, and then repulsed during the Bush-Cheney years, are reasonable and in the national interest. Hence, for starters, reasonable gun control would involve: 1) returning to earlier attempts to require child-safety locks on handguns; 2) increasing the minimum age for gun purchases; 3) requiring stricter background checks on weapons purchased; 4) producing better data sharing among police, legal, and mental health institutions and universities; and 5) closing the gun show loophole through which guns can be purchased without background checks."

The Virginia Tech Canard

Following the slaughter at Virginia Tech, the Governor set up a blue ribbon panel to analyze the rampage. The net result was a badly flawed report. It did not address the problems central to the causes behind the shooting. The third and final version of the report, known as *The Addendum*, shies away from making the tough recommendations needed to get at the heart of the problem and prevent future shootings on school grounds.

Unlike Colorado's Columbine report, which was written by the panel members who analyzed the shooting, Virginia hired a firm doing business with the state (Arlington-based *TriData*) to do the drafting, which was a conflict of interest. *TriData* was paid around $700,000. Virginia bought and paid for the report it wanted; a report analyzing the tragedy in such a way to gloss over incompetence and call no one's actions or inactions into question.

I have read the report several times and each time I come away scratching my head. The sheer size of the report is noteworthy, but its failure to face up to what needs to be done—hold people accountable for their actions and inactions—makes *The Addendum* an exercise in futility.

The report did not address issues such as identifying mistakes in judgment and the individuals who should be held accountable for their actions or inactions. Indeed, the report is an amazing exercise in avoiding accountability and legal liability.

The investigating panel should have written the report in order to avoid any hint of conflict of interest. A state panel examined the behavior of state employees and the state's largest university to determine if there was any malfeasance, but not one member of the victims' families was a panel member. The state did pay for a family representative and spokesperson on the panel. But, who was paying the representative and to whom did the representative owe loyalty? The state—again, a conflict of interest that is hardly conducive to impartiality.

Several key players declined to cooperate with the review panel. The lack of cooperation is disheartening and puzzling. Specifically, the Virginia State Police, the ATF, and the gun dealers "declined to provide the panel with copies of the applications" Seung Hui Cho completed when he bought the weapons that would eventually kill over thirty innocent people. The report notes "the Virginia State Police ... did describe the contents of Cho's gun purchase applications to members of the panel and its staff." The state police's willingness to "describe" is a limp attempt to explain their failure to cooperate and provide the panel with documents. This lack of cooperation is a lethal flaw in the report—it is inexcusable.

The panel was impeded in its work by the FOIA rules that did not allow more than two members to meet together or speak by phone without it being considered a public meeting. This is bureaucracy at its worst. The report needs to be more specific in detailing the problems this bureaucratic obstacle presented.

The report sugarcoats glaring errors and problems. For example, the report on page 10, talks about the findings and recommendations in the report being two different kinds. One, "What was done well," and two, "What could have been done better." The report should have exposed people in positions of authority failing to do their jobs—"could have been done better" is backing away from holding individuals and institutions accountable for their actions.

In this same vein, the report says:

- The police may have made an error in reaching the premature conclusion

- Their initial lead was a good one; and,

- The person of interest was probably not on campus.

The Virginia Tech Police *did make* a very serious error by jumping to a premature conclusion and giving the wrong impression to school officials. This error should never be glossed over.

The report appears to make excuses for the failure of the university's Policy Group to put out a campus-wide alert following the discovery of the first two bodies. The previous August, the university had alerted the campus when a convict named William Morva had escaped from a nearby prison and killed a law enforcement officer and a guard. The alert indicated the murderer was on the loose and could be on campus. The university set its own standard in August of 2006 by issuing an alert, and then violated the standard in April 2007. Lives would have been saved had an alert gone out; the report skirts around this critical point.

In sum, *The Addendum* fails to do its job in critical areas; it is bland, and raises no real red flags. The report is the equivalent of reading a book with no thesis. The recommendations indicate what "should" be done. The "shoulds" relate to such things as analyzing, training, complying with an act, police being members of panels, etc. Yes, these "shoulds" need to be done. But, nowhere does the report say individuals should be held accountable for their actions or inactions; organizations and individuals must be liable when they break their own standards and over 30 lives are lost.

One member of the Panel reported the panel members felt under pressure to produce a report that would not lead to litigation.

The report may be impressive in size, but it is unimpressive in content. The report falls short of what it needed to do…make clear everyone in a position of responsibility must be held to standards of safety and failure to meet those standards will result in stiff penalties. Instead, readers are left wandering from page to page in an effort to tie ends together and make these conclusions for themselves.

The America
We All Want

Part 4

Taking control in our
communities

Chapter 11

What Parents Can Do

Here is a place to start. If you are getting ready to send your daughter or son to college, part of your selection process should be to familiarize yourself with the prospective school's security procedures, policies, and emergency plans.

For those of you sending a student to school in Virginia these questions are extremely important. I have lived in Virginia for over forty years and all three of my sons went to Virginia colleges and universities. If I were selecting schools for my children today, I would probably not select a Virginia school because of the poor state of campus security—compared to other states. Compounding the problem in Virginia is the fact the state's legal system operates under the doctrine of Sovereign Immunity—meaning you have little or no legal recourse against a state school even in cases of clear negligence.

Virginia is one of the most difficult states to prove premises liability or hold anybody liable for incompetence. Therefore, a student killed or hurt by someone on school grounds in *The Old Dominion* may avoid prosecution based upon this mindset. If you are sending a son or daughter to a college or university, you may be doing so at a terrible risk.

As noted earlier in this book, the Virginia Supreme Court, time and time again, refuses to recognize the responsibility of a business proprietor to protect "its invitees from unreasonable risk of physical harm." The whole question of "foreseeability" is hard to pin down. But the Supreme Courts of other states do recognize there is a point where a proprietor can be held responsible for not taking action to protect "its invitees." Courts in other states do recognize there comes a point when violent behavior is predictable and a proprietor can be held responsible for ignoring the warning signs.

Ask Questions

The following are some questions to ask school officials:

- Does the school have a plan in place identifying aberrant behavior, and what steps will the school take to remove potentially dangerous individuals from the campus?

- Does the school regularly review and update its security procedures?

- Has the school brought the students into the dialog on what should be done in the case of an emergency?

- Does the school have a campus-wide warning system in place, such as sirens, text messaging, and cell phone warnings?

- What is the relationship between campus security and the local and state police? How closely do they cooperate and do they have a coordinated emergency plan?

- What would happen to a student if he or she were found to have a weapon on campus?

- How does the school define weapons?

- How quickly can campus security lock down or secure all buildings on campus?

- What is the school's policy on bringing guns (or any weapon including sling shots) onto campus?

- What is the school's policy if a student is caught sending harassing or threatening emails to someone?

- Can a student, staff, or faculty member be directed to seek a psychological evaluation and treatment?

- How quickly are parents notified if a student is causing a problem or disturbance—or appears to be exhibiting behavior others consider threatening?

- Do the campus police or security officials have the right to move immediately on an individual who's threatening behavior alarms students, faculty, or staff? <u>If not, do not enroll your child in that school</u>.

Exemplary Policy - Who is Doing It Right?

Several years ago I spent nearly an hour discussing campus security with the Chief of University Police, State University of New York—Oneonta (SUNY—Oneonta). What I learned was impressive. If every school in this country had a well thought out and run security plan like the one at Oneonta, our school grounds would be far, far safer places.

The campus security at SUNY-Oneonta is a police department; therefore its officers carry weapons. The Regional Police Academy is tied to the campus police department. The academy runs a wide variety of specialized law enforcement courses, trains new officers, and trains officers to be instructors.

SUNY-Oneonta campus has had an emergency plan in place since 1994, but since the tragedy at Virginia Tech, the school has tightened and improved campus security. The chief began by telling me it is against the law to bring a weapon of any kind on a school campus in New York. This law covers both state and private schools. Indeed, every state university in New York is required to have an emergency plan in place, and the Oneonta and Binghamton campuses are the first to meet the state's standard for security. Highlights of the SUNY—Oneonta plan include:

- The ability to lock down every building on campus (with the exception of the gym) with four strokes on the computer keyboard. There is a radio system in all buildings for emergency use.

- Blue prints of all campus buildings are on hand in police headquarters in case of an emergency.

- A Behavioral Assessment Team meets every week to discuss student problems and activities. The group is made up of the campus Chief of Police, the Director of Counseling, the Director of Residence Life, the Associate Vice President for Judicial Affairs, the Vice President of Student Development, and the Health Center Director.

- The Chief of Police has the power to act immediately and to take whatever action he deems necessary if an individual is thought to be a danger to himself/herself or others.

- A campus-wide siren for notification there is an emergency on campus.

- The school has the ability to notify all students, staff, and faculty of an emergency through NY ALERT—a cell phone/email/text messaging system. All New York State University campuses will have this system within the near future.

- SUNY—Oneonta will soon have in place a video and card access system for all campus buildings.

- SUNY—Oneonta has bought and installed a sophisticated key system for all buildings. The keys cannot be duplicated.

- The school gives its officers extensive training through a variety of courses including *Active Shooter Course* and *Patrol Officers Course.*

- SUNY—Oneonta has hired a full-time Emergency Management Coordinator.

- The school is linked to major criminal data bases in Albany.

- The school regularly reviews its crime prevention security analysis for all campus buildings.

- The University Police Department has an ambulance on hand, on campus.

- New York state law required all university police departments on state affiliated schools must have a Memorandum of Understanding with the state police on immediate emergency response responsibilities and actions. SUNY-Oneonta has such a memorandum and maintains close ties with the New York State Police and the city of Oneonta Police Department.

- Students are given a full security briefing as part of their campus orientation.

- Each staff and faculty member has at her or his desk a bright orange Crisis Management folder for immediate and easy reference. The folder contains phone numbers and contacts. The subjects covered are:

- Emergency Responses—Shelter in Place, Notification, and Building Evacuation.

- Reporting an Emergency on Campus—Bomb Threat, Fire, Accident or Medical Emergency.

- Threats of Physical Harm from a Person or Persons—Threats by Email, Text Message, Phone, or Note—Threatening or Aggressive Behavior, and Policies and Procedures.

- Student Emergencies—Disturbed or Disturbing Emotional Behavior, Serious Illness or Injury, Threatening or Irrational Behavior, Crime in Progress or has been Committed, and Sexual Assault.

- Non-Emergency Student Problems—Disturbed or Disturbing Emotional Behavior, Illness or Injury, and Learning, Psychological, or Physical Disability.

Inept Virginia

The state of Virginia points to the millions of dollars it has spent on security systems as proof Virginia schools are safe. Yes, Richmond has spent hundreds of millions of dollars on electronic security systems; yes, it has developed new security procedures. What Virginia officials don't say is everything was in place on April 16, 2007 to prevent the slaughter of 30 people and wounding of 17 others in Norris Hall. No new electronic security system was needed.

What Virginia state officials fail to mention is no one was ever held accountable for incompetence; failing to initiate the warning and lockdown.

The flaw is always the human factor. Spending additional funds on security is not the answer. Until someone is held accountable for his or her actions or inactions leading to mass murder, the state's schools will not be measurably safer.

So, what should be done in Virginia to prevent another Appalachian School of Law slaughter or a repeat of the April 16, 2007 tragedy at Blacksburg? A great deal, and here are three places to start:

First, the Virginia legislature should adopt a law stating if a faculty or staff member identifies a student as mentally unbalanced and potentially violent, the student must be referred to mental health authorities for evaluation. At the same time an alert should be issued to all gun stores banning the sale of weapons and ammunition to this individual. Any person selling a gun to someone for whom a warning has been issued should serve a mandatory, long jail sentence.

Second—and by law—all educational facilities in Virginia, both public and private, should have in place a mandatory emergency plan. All presidents of the state's colleges and universities should be required to annually read and understand their school's security plans, and to sign confirming they have done so.

Third, in the event of any shooting on or near school grounds, the school should immediately lockdown. Police should be called and posted around the facility until it is clear the shooter has been captured.

What It Will Take

What will it take stop the increase in gun violence on school grounds and begin to reverse the numbers of shooting incidents?

Quite simply it begins with good people speaking out against extreme gun-rights advocates. Specifically, actions such as the National Rifle Association's (NRA) excursion into paranoid lunacy—a world of complete unfettered access to all guns.

The NRA's latest excursion into mind control and violation of the constitutional right of freedom of speech centers on it's efforts to get states to adopt laws making it illegal for doctors to ask patients if they have a gun at home. According to *USA Today*, three states are considering laws to penalize doctors and other health care providers for asking patients or their parents whether they have a gun at home.

> *"The National Rifle Association and other pro-gun interest groups argue doctors violate patients; second amendment right to keep and bear arms by inquiring about gun ownership. Doctors say they ask only because of safety concerns. Prohibiting them from asking about guns violates the first amendment, at least one constitutional law expert says."*

What about the right of any doctor to ask any patient any question pertaining to the patient's wellbeing? Apparently the NRA believes there is only one amendment in the Bill of Rights, the Second Amendment. If you are going to apply order of importance to the amendments, then it is not unreasonable to think the most important consideration on the founding fathers' minds was freedom of speech. The last time I counted "one" came before "two."

What a shame if the power of the gun lobby, coupled with the cowardice of the politicians, rewrites history and interprets the *Constitution* to the benefit of the paranoid few and the profits of gun manufacturers and the NRA.

What will it take to stop the blood baths on our school grounds? As a beginning, it will take people such as you demanding action along the lines outlined in this chapter.

Chapter 12

Think Local And State.

It is no secret our elected officials in Washington are so dysfunctional. Very little is accomplished. Even relatively mundane bills are hard to pass.

At the heart of the problem is the fact we are dealing with unscrupulous people whose sole goal is to make money no matter how many people are killed along the way. For them, the ends justify the means.

The Lie

There is a saying: *if you tell a lie long enough it becomes the truth.*

The Big Lie: "They are coming to get your guns."

We are dealing with such a lie. The National Rifle Association and gun manufacturers repeat the mantra: They are coming to get your guns.

Who is the "they?"

If you ask those who are repeating this Gregorian nonsense-chant, you get either a blank stare or simply "the government." As I write this book, the "they" almost always refers to the government as a whole or some unnamed shadowy part of the federal government.

Ok, the government. But this is a huge country. It would take the whole government to carry out such a plan.

There are approximately 2.7 million federal workers. Are you telling me they are going to leave their jobs and go door to door searching for guns to confiscate? Really? Do you have any idea how long it would take 2.7 million people to search the homes of 330 million Americans? Furthermore, who will be left to provide the federal services we all rely on?

If by some incredibly remote chance these paranoid gun-toting U.S. citizens are right, it would mean no one would be left to send you your social security check much less run the Defense Department or any other federal agency. This country will be vulnerable to a foreign take-over. If the chanting automatons are right, we all may be learning to speak Chinese soon.

I don't think those who fall prey to the "they're coming to take your guns" look at the illogic of what they are saying, nor do they recognize they are being duped.

The Facts

Here are the facts as they relate to gun violence in the United States:

- Greed as well as personal and career interests have turned our House and Senate into malfunctioning elected bodies. Our legislators are all too easy prey for lobbyists and interests groups with plenty of cash and perks to buy the politicians. Given this state of affairs, it is next to impossible to get federal level elected officials to turn their attention to finding ways to curb gun violence.

- Every day 90 Americans are killed by guns, according the Brady Campaign. Every day nine children are killed or wounded by guns. But not even these frightening figures are strong enough to spur Congress to look at ways to curb gun violence.

- The only piece of legislation in 2014 dealing with gun safety and passed by both the House and the Senate was a comprehensive and bipartisan background check bill in April, 2014.

- Nationwide, gun homicides have declined in recent years, but cities' gun deaths rates have remained significantly higher than the rest of the country. Furthermore, the number of mass shootings, particularly school shootings, has increased at an alarming rate.

According to the Brady Campaign:

- One in three Americans knows someone who has been shot.

- On average, 31 Americans are murdered with guns every day and 151 are treated for a gun assault in an emergency room.

- Every day on average, 55 people kill themselves with a firearm, and 46 people are shot or killed by accident with a gun.

There is some hope to prevent the carnage. Positive steps to curb the gun violence have been adopted by many states and communities.

Forget About Congress

It is clear solutions to ending carnage will have to be found some place other than in the halls of Congress. We are not going to change policies toward guns in the U.S. Congress; Capital Hill is too corrupted by lobbyists, the NRA, and gun manufacturers, all of whom share the goal of selling as many guns as possible—no matter what the resulting cost in human lives.

We are going to have to look at local and state governments to make progress in curbing gun violence. And, here there is some good news. We are also going to have a more sophisticated approach to curbing gun violence. The solution cannot be one size fits all. Gun laws need to reflect the needs of various communities. For starters, I believe gun policies need to be different in rural areas from those in metropolitan areas. This fact is another reason why we cannot expect a solution to the carnage at the federal level.

For example, I live in Kilmarnock, a small town in rural Virginia, where almost everybody owns a gun and hunting is a way of life. The town council, in March 2016, unanimously passed an amended ordinance making the discharge of a gun, rifle, pistol or other firearm a Class 1 misdemeanor. The town council's actions show we can work together to make our communities safer by trying to prevent the reckless use of firearms. The amended ordinance also demonstrates laws can be passed in no way undercutting the Second Amendment.

Action at the Local Level

Throughout the country local and state politicians seem to be responding to growing public frustration over the slaughter on our school grounds and they are taking action. For example, Louisiana, Minnesota, New Hampshire, Vermont, Washington, and Wisconsin have passed laws to remove firearms from criminals' hands. In California, after the shooting at Isla Vista, Governor Jerry Brown signed into law a measure allowing authorities or family members to more easily get restraining orders against people who pose a significant threat.

Prior to the Sandy Hook tragedy only two states, California and Rhode Island, had laws requiring background checks on gun sales. Since then, the number has risen to seven and now includes in addition to California and Rhode Island, Connecticut, Colorado, Delaware, New York, and Washington. And, since the horror at Sandy Hook, 37 states have passed a total of 99 laws strengthening gun regulations.

In August 2015, Massachusetts Governor Duval Patrick signed into law a gun-safety bill granting police chiefs the authority to prevent certain individuals from getting firearms licenses.

In Sunny Vale, California voters approved a measure designed to discourage straw gun purchases, where one person buys a gun for someone else.

There is a growing chorus of voices to stop the gun-violence madness.

The Road Ahead

Clearly, there is a path forward, and it is at the state and local level.

You, the reader, can make a difference by joining the growing number of voices of concerned Americans demanding some measures to curb the slaughter. It will take thought; imagination, patience, and determination to make our lives safer.

More and more, people are finding ways to keep firearms out of public venues. *Moms Demand Action* has taken the gun issue to large retailers and is asking large them to prohibit customers from carrying guns into their locations. The threat of a boycott gets businesses attention. *Moms Demand Action* has been successful with Starbucks, Target, Chipotle, Jack in the Box, and Sonic Drive-In, just to mention a few.

Curbing gun violence has made progress, albeit it is slow, at the state and local levels. Here is one more example before I close this chapter; Washington State passed Initiative 594 by a wide margin. The measure requires criminal background checks on all firearms sales and transfers in the state including at gun shows and on the Internet.

Initiative 594 does not undercut one aspect of the Second Amendment; it should be adopted in all 50 states. If 594 had been in place in 2007 in Virginia, Seung-Hui Cho almost certainly would not have been able to buy a gun and slaughter 32 people and wound 17 others at Virginia Tech.

Chapter 13

Creative Approaches

Imagination and Initiative

Mayor Steven Fulop of Jersey City, New Jersey used the city's police department's need to buy $350,000 in firearms and ammunition as a way to influence gun suppliers. To bid on the contract, the companies had to explain what they do with old weapons and how they comply with federal and state background check laws.

The mayor's policy was meant to encourage the private sector to clamp down on both illegal and straw purchases, both of which are major ways criminals get guns.

Peace Fellowship

Richmond, California has implemented a plan to curb gun violence. The plan looks at the individuals, not the weapons, to find a solution. DeVonne Boggan, director of neighborhood safety for the city, believes the solution is to find ways to convince young men not to pick up guns in the first place; not to turn to firearms to solve their problems.

Here is how it works. Boggan's office identifies young men who are suspected of being involved in a shooting, but who have not been charged or convicted. He invites them to join "The Peace Fellowship Program."

The program involves a team of older neighborhood residents who coach the young men in setting goals and the steps they need to take to achieve them. These goals range from getting driver's licenses to applying for college.

Boggan's program to end gun violence began in 2007 and as of July 2014 had recruited 68 peace fellows. Twenty-five of these young men have completed the fifteen-month program. Fifty-seven have avoided being charged with a firearm assault since joining and all but three are still alive.

The program's perks include trips abroad to Cape Town and Dubai and cash awards for staying in the program for more than six months.

The Peace Fellowship Program appears to have had real success. In January 2014, the police department announced Richmond had the lowest number of homicides in three decades.

What You Can Do

Here are some suggestions to help make our schools, theaters, shopping malls, and entire communities safe.

First, do not use the words "gun control."

You fall right into the NRA trap when you do. The NRA has tainted those words and turned them into a highly charged indictment of people whom the NRA claims are trying to destroy Constitutional rights.

Nothing could be further from the truth. You are trying to protect the rights granted us in the Constitution. You cannot exercise the right of free speech or the right to vote, if you are dead; if you have been gunned down. You are not trying to control guns, you are trying to keep them away from people who will harm others. Stress your support of hunting and the rights guaranteed to all Americans by the Second Amendment.

Second, exercise your Constitutional right to freedom of speech.

Speak out at every turn in an effort to keep guns out of the hands of those who are a threat to themselves and others, terrorists, convicted felons, and domestic abusers. Write letters to the editor calling for sensible legislation to keep our schools and communities safe and free from gun violence. When you write, make sure you affirm you are doing so in doing so in accordance with the Second Amendment. Support candidates who are willing to stand up to the NRA and gun lobby.

Third, demand all candidates running for office explain their positions on gun laws.

Pressure on locally elected officials to adopt sensible gun safety laws can work and a full explanation on where they stand on this critical issue can help make them accountable.

Fourth, require background checks for all sales and purchases of guns in your state or community.

The local sheriff, police, or constable can and should be entrusted with this responsibility. These offices issue the carry permits. No one should be given a permit without a background check. The background check should be the equivalent to the no-fly list. In other words, people who are convicted felons, have been deemed a threat to themselves and others, terrorists, and domestic abusers should not be allowed to buy a weapon.

Fifth, ban the sale of military-style, semiautomatic assault weapons

Ban the sale of military-style, semiautomatic assault weapons capable of shooting more than 10 rounds of ammunition without reloading.

Sixth, increase funding for public schools to hire additional school resource and security officers.

School resource officers are in a unique position to identify students who are under stress and are potentially violent. Increased, armed security officers can act as a deterrent to potential shooters

Seventh, conduct regular gun buy-back campaigns; at least once a year.

As noted earlier, gun buy-back campaigns have been a success and have played a key role and taking illegal guns off the street

Eight, require that every public school train and arm at least one staff member with a gun.

Having every public school train at least one staff member with a gun (and keeping the identity of the individual a secret) can play a critical role in saving lives. The key is making sure the person is vetted, trained ,and is known to law enforcement authorities.

Ninth and finally, as I mentioned above, do not use the words "gun control."

We have a long way to go before we can begin to significantly curb gun violence. The road ahead will not be easy and interest groups who oppose measures to make us safer are richer beyond imagination. They are willing to use that money to do anything and everything to stop measures to curb gun violence.

Don't Be Afraid

A lawyer in Richmond, Virginia told me the people behind Virginia Tech are powerful and vindictive. He had dealt with them. To paraphrase him, he said the Tech backers will seek to punish me for exposing the lies and deceit in your analysis of the shooting. He said everything I wrote was true, but they have the money to take me to court and bleed you dry. They will try to take everything from you.

A professor at the University of Richmond asked me if I carry a gun. When I told him no, he said you should, "You don't know what your are dealing with. Please be careful."

A resident of southwestern Virginia phoned my home to warn me. "You have offended powerful people. We have deep abandoned mine shafts and people can disappear."

A good friend of mine jokingly suggested I get a remote starter for my car and not make any dinner reservations in Blacksburg.

When a TV station in Richmond carried a review of my book on the Virginia Tech tragedy a man threatened to beat me up. The fact he had never read the book didn't seem to bother him. Nor was he concerned about the First Amendment.

The United Kingdom

There is strong evidence of successful gun legislation elsewhere. The United Kingdom and Australia for example, has dramatically reduced gun violence.

More than 15 years ago, the United Kingdom enacted the *UK's Firearms Act*, preventing private citizens from owning most types of handguns and making it much harder to purchase other types of guns, such as rifles and shotguns. *The Firearms Act* came nine years after

Parliament had passed another gun control law making semiautomatic weapons illegal. In the last 15 years, "more than 200,000 guns and 700 tons of ammunition have been taken off the streets." Statistics indicate the number of gun crimes initially increased, but by 2005 a decline began continuing to this day thanks to strict enforcement and regular police sweeps.

UK Mass Killing Prompted Action

Both British laws were enacted in response to mass shootings, with the Firearms Act motivated by a 1996 primary school massacre leaving 16 5- and 6-year-olds dead. Gun restrictions are in place in the UK, and it is a democracy.

Today, according to the press, most gun crime in the UK can be traced back to fewer than 1,000 illegal weapons still in circulation. The laws have been so successful anyone looking to get a gun will find himself or herself resorting to rebuilt antique weapons, homemade bullets and even illicit "rent-a-gun" schemes.

CNN reports gun crime in England and Wales, in the late '90s, following the passage of the law, peaking at 24,094 incidents in 2003–04. But 2010–2011 gun crime had decreased by 53 percent from high.

Australia

The United Kingdom is not the only country to adopt affective measures to guard against gun violence.

On April 28, 1996, a gunman opened fire on tourists in a seaside resort in Port Arthur, Tasmania. He killed 35 people and wounded 23 more; the worst mass murder in Australia's history.

Twelve days later, Australia's government acted. Led by newly elected conservative Prime Minister John Howard, it announced a bipartisan deal with state and local governments to enact sweeping measures to keep firearms out of the hands of people who are a threat to themselves and others. The results of these policy changes are clear: They have worked well.

At the heart of the push was a massive buyback of more than 600,000 semi-automatic shotguns and rifles. That figure amounted to approximately one-fifth of all firearms in circulation in Australia. The Australian laws also prohibited private sales, requiring all weapons be individually registered to their owners, and requiring all gun buyers present a "genuine reason" for needing each weapon at the time of the purchase. Interestingly, self-defense was not considered a valid reason to buy a weapon. In the wake of the tragedy, polls showed public support for these measures at upwards of 90 percent.

According the *New York Magazine,* "in the decade after the (Australian) law was introduced, the firearm homicide rate dropped by 59 per cent and the firearm suicide rate fell by 65 per cent, with no corresponding increase in homicides and suicides committed without guns."

Evil Exists Because Good People Remain Silent.

Common sense has led to some progress in the U.S. The fear of all families that a child might be gunned down at school appears to be uniting support from people of all political stripes, Republicans, Democrats, Tea Party, Green Party, and Environmentalists, to do something to curb violence in America. And that is the key to success. All of us need to put our other political differences aside and work together.

The argument made by some that keeping guns out of the hands of people who are a threat to society is the first step toward taking away all our rights is simply not true.

First, there are restrictions on all the Amendments to the Constitution. I cannot use foul language in public; I cannot threaten people by written or spoken word. There are restrictions on all rights for the public good. The unfettered acquisition of guns and the resulting mass murders, are not in the common good. The radical interpretation of the Second Amendment has resulted in undermining the rights granted to all of use in the Constitution.

Second, other democracies thrive with strict public safety laws concerning guns.

Third, yes, we will never be completely free of shootings, but just as Australia and the United Kingdom, we can significantly reduce the instances of gun violence by making our voices heard.

Speak Out

All of us must find ways to speak out to protect our children, spouses, and fellow citizens. The America we want is an America where children go to school free of fear for their lives, where people, can go to the movies without watching for a shooter, and where professors and teachers can enter a classroom without thinking *will this be the day someone brings a gun in and kills us all?*

Index

A

ACLU 74
Addendum, The 106, 107, 108
Allen, George 96
al Qa'ida 54, 56
Ahrens, Lorne 19
American Civil Liberties Union 74
Appalachian School of Law 5, 7, 9, 8, 27, 44, 45, 47, 58, 60, 67, 81, 83, 84, 91, 98, 99, 118
ATF 56, 107
Aurora, Colorado 67, 68
Australia 15, 36, 136, 137, 138

B

Bastrop, Texas 55, 56
Baton Rouge, Louisiana 19
Bean, Carl 45
Betzel, Dr. Cathye 59
Black Lives Matter 19, 21
Blacksburg, Virginia 35, 59, 70, 72, 73, 76, 118, 135
Boehner, John 49
Boggan, DeVonne 131, 132
Boston Globe 55
Boston Marathon 43
Brady Center 67
Breivik, Anders Behring 15
Briston, Rumain 22

Brown, Michael 22, 126
BTP Arms 68
Bush, Jeb 34
Burson-Marsteller 8

C

Canada 6, 15
Canons of Judicial Conduct for the State of Virginia 70
Cariens, Janice 5
Carilion St. Albans Psychiatric Hospital 46
Castile, Philandro 19
CENTCOM 95
Charleston, South Carolina 28
Cheney, Vice President Dick 106
Chesapeake Bay Writers 5
Chicago Tribune 55
Chipotle 127
Chronicle of Higher Education 88
CIA 96, 108
Clery Act , The 99
Cleveland, Ohio 20, 21, 22
CNN 42, 137
Columbine 8, 35, 42, 43, 83, 106
Columbine effect 42
Crannis, Blacksburg Police Chief Kim 70, 72, 76
Cuccinelli, Virginia Attorney General Ken 69

D

DAISH 5, 6, 16, 95
Dales, Angela 5, 7, 27, 28, 60, 67, 87
Dales , Danny 7
Deeds, Austin 85
Deeds, Senator Creigh 35, 85
de Haven, Professor Helen 96
Democrat 3
Dickinson, Laura 98, 99
Director of National Intelligence 95
Dowd, John E. Eastern Michigan University 65
Duval, Massachusetts Governor Patrick 126

E

Eastern Michigan University 98

Economist 48
Emergency Custody Order 85

F

Falco, Ed 45
Falcon Heights, Minnesota 19
FBI 23, 42, 78
Firearms Act 136
Firestorm 8, 82
Flinchum, Virginia Tech Police Chief Wendell 59, 70, 72, 73, 76, 88
FOIA 107
Freeh, Louis 97
Fulop, Mayor 131

G

Garner, Eric 22
Gerald, Matthew 20
Ghawi, Jessica 68
Giovanni, Nikke 45
Governor's Review Panel Report, 59
Greek financial crisis 56
Grundy, Virginia 35
Guys and Guns Run Amock, 48

H

Harris, Eric 15, 43
Harris, Robert Q. 75
Herring, Virginia Attorney General 76
Hicok, Bob 45
Hokie Spirit Memorial Fund 83, 84
Holmes, James 54, 68
Howard, Prime Minister John 137

I

Imperial Japan 6
Independence, Ohio 21
ISIL 5, 6, 16, 56, 95
Isla Vista, California 8, 27

J

Jack in the Box 127

Jackson, Montaell 20
Jersey City, New Jersey 131
Johnson, Micah Xavier 18
Journal of College and University Law, The 96
Judicial Inquiry and Review Commission, 79

K

Kellner, Dylon 48, 105
Klebold, Douglas 43
Kristof, Nicholas 105
Krol, Michael L 19

L

LaDue 43
Lanza, Adam 14, 43, 53, 54
Lewis, Mary Ann, Associate Dean 46
Loehmann, Timothy 21
Lone Wolf 13, 14, 15, 16, 17, 18, 19
Long, Gavin 19
Louisiana 19, 126
Lucky Gunner 68
Lyons , 6 Northumberland County Sheriff James R "Doc"

M

MACV 96
Malvo, Lee Boyd 15
Marshall Plan, The 7
Matsch, Senior U.S. Judge Richard P 68
McCranie, Lancaster County Sheriff Patrick 6
McDonnell, Virginia Governor Bob 86
Mexico 6
Minnesota 19, 43, 126
Montrell Jackson 20
Morva, William 73, 108
Mother Jones 28, 42, 44
Muhammad, John Allen 15

N

National Law Enforcement Memorial Fund 17
National Review, The 86, 87
National Rifle Association 14, 67, 119, 123
Nazi Germany 6

New Hampshire 126
New York Times 95, 105
None So Blind 96
Norris Hall 73, 74, 88, 89, 118
Norris, Lisa 46
Northern Arizona University 28
NRA (Also See National Rifle Association)35, 55, 67, 68, 119, 120, 125, 132, 133

O

Obama 55, 56, 95
Odighizuwa 14, 44

P

Pape 56
Parker 96, 97
Peace Fellowship Program 131, 132
Penn State 97, 98
Phillips 67, 68
Powell, Justice Cleo E. 70, 74, 76
Pryde 59, 69, 72, 76, 77, 83, 89

R

Rappatomac Writers 5
Republican 3
Rice, Tamir 20, 21, 22
Richmond, California 131
Roseburg, Oregon 27, 28
Roy, Professor Lucinda 59

S

Saigon 96
Sandy Hook 8, 27, 28, 83, 126
Second Amendment, The 14, 31, 33, 34, 41, 53, 54, 55, 57, 58, 119, 126, 127, 133, 138
Seung Hui Cho 14, 15, 45, 46, 54, 85, 88, 107
Scott, Walter 22
Smith, Michael 19
Sonic Drive-In 127
South Vietnam 96
Sportsman Guide 68
Starbucks 127
Steger, Charles 88

Sterling, Alton 19
SUNY-Oneonta 115, 117

T

Target 127
Taylor III, Orange 98, 99
Tea Party 3, 138
Texas Southern University 28
Thompson, Brent 19
TriData 83, 106

U

Umpqua Community College 27, 28
United Kingdom 15, 136, 137, 138
University of Richmond 135
University of Tennessee 96
U.S. Central Command 95
U.S. Congress 125
U.S. Military Assistance Command, Vietnam (MACV) 96
Utoya Island 16

V

Vermont 126
Viet Cong 96
Vietnam 6, 96
Virginia State Police 107
Virginia Supreme Court 8, 69, 72, 74, 75, 76, 77, 78, 83, 113
Virginia Tech 7, 8, 9, 8, 27, 35, 36, 45, 46, 47, 58, 59, 60, 69, 70, 72, 73, 74, 76, 77,
    82, 83, 84, 86, 88, 93, 97, 98, 99, 106, 108, 115, 127, 135

W

Wascea, Minnesota 43
Washington 6, 7, 15, 56, 57, 78, 121, 126, 127
Webb, Lancaster County Deputy Sheriff William 6
West Ambler Johnston Hall 59, 88, 98
Whitman, Charles Joseph 13, 16
Wisconsin 126
World War II 6

Z

Zamarripa, PA 19

About the Author

David Cariens is a retired CIA officer who currently teaches intelligence analysis and writing in the U.S. and abroad. He is the author of *A Question of Accountability: The Murder of Angela Dales* — an examination of the shooting at the Appalachian School of Law in Grundy, Virginia and a textbook, *Critical Thinking Through Writing: Intelligence and Crime Analysis*. Cariens also wrote an analysis of the Virginia Tech rampage entitle, *Virginia Tech: Make Sure it Doesn't Get Out*. He contributed to the International Association of Law Enforcement Intelligence Agency's *Criminal Intelligence for the 21st Century*.

Made in the USA
Middletown, DE
08 July 2019